"Progress is impossible without change, and those who cannot change their minds cannot change anything. "

- George Bernard Shaw

Contents

Acknowledgements

This book has my name on the front cover but it is the hard work of many people that has made its existence possible. No person stands alone in this world, there are always other people in one's life that influence your thinking and actions. I present this work as a token of my appreciation of everyone that instructed and helped me along my path. From learning about business systems and the application of lean principles to seeing and understanding the human side of work processes and how they affect people.

I have made it an important part of my life's journey to try to interpret and understand the human element of business practices. In the time I have been doing this I have developed a pragmatic approach to problem solving and discovering solutions to eliminate difficult issues. People are not the problem, it is the system they work in that creates the problem. When business processes are broken, how can anyone blame the employees when things go wrong?

As someone that was challenged in school to achieve the best grades, I developed an understanding of how my brain interprets real-life situations and I found that I recognize patterns. Therefore, I attribute my success in business management and as a lean consultant to my ability to identify specific patterns of behavior. I never place any judgments on the behavior I observe, I only determine if the practices that are supported by the observed behavior are effective in achieving the desired business goals and objectives.

I want to thank my mother, Aileen Turner for introducing me to the art of critical thinking and problem solving. Little did she know how effective it would be in my professional career.

I want to thank my father, William Turner for giving me the best advice about data, information, and life: "Believe nothing you hear and only half of what you see." I use this every time I start a new project. We love you Dad, and miss you every day since your passing.

I thank my wife Jodine for her patience, love and support during the late hours I spent alone in my office converting my thoughts into words that were eventually used to create this book. She is my soul mate, an inspiration and the best mentor of all. I love you, always and forever!

I want to take this opportunity to thank my daughter, Gemma and her four children for their support and love. I am the proudest father and grandfather on the planet.

I want to acknowledge all the earlier pioneers that have gone before me. They strived to discover the creativity that lies dormant in the human mind. Their work created a solid foundation, which allowed me to build upon it and to discover other possibilities.

Chapter 1

Introduction

Why are lean principles or thinking becoming so prevalent in modern business practices?

To remain a competitive, agile, and low cost producer, a business must start to focus on identifying and eliminating waste. Being able to do this in a consistent and sustainable way is crucial to the survival of any business that wants to thrive in the global economy of the 21st century.

Lean principles or thinking is exactly what the name sounds like – it is about leaning out an organization's processes through the identification and elimination of waste. Some of the more unsavory sounding descriptions for lean methodologies are 'cutting to the bone', 'trimming the fat,' and 'lean and mean' which are euphemisms encouraging employees work harder.

I personally do not support these terms because they misrepresent and undermine the concept and purpose of lean principles. I prefer the English term "Just in Time," which is loosely translated from the Japanese term "Kanban Seido." Why do I prefer this name instead of lean principles? Well, I prefer it because it defines the original concept of the continuous process improvement methods based on the Toyota Production System (TPS).

A business must focus their resources on getting the right things, to the right place, at the right time, to deliver the right products or services to the customers on time, every time. Inherent within the phrase 'Just in Time' is the need to establish a consistent and repeatable level of quality and speed. However, because the phrase "Lean principles" is now ingrained in the world-wide business vocabulary, I will use this term throughout the rest of this book.

Authors Womack and Jones define lean thinking as a series or collection of 'tools' that you can unleash in your business to reduce cost and waste, and deliver a consistent and effective service that increases value for your customers. It is about creating a vision and using the lean tools to reduce variability and cut out waste, being efficient and running a smooth, competitive, and profitable operation.

Pioneers like Henry Ford championed lean thinking and it was adopted by the Japanese automakers Toyota as the principle upon which they have been able to build, operate, and grow their businesses. It was not until much later that the Western business world realized the value and potential of this approach to their respective organizations and operations.

Some refer to lean principles as the Toyota Production System, or JIT (just-in-time) manufacturing, which focuses on things like continuous flow production systems, value streams, and pull systems using Kanban (all of which we will get to later). In an organization that has decided to implement lean principles, they need to take careful notice of a few important factors. Lean principles require a paradigm shift to introduce a new approach that includes discipline, planning, execution, standardization and feedback. Without these, an organization will not be capable of implementing and sustaining a Lean Management System over the long term.

A Lean Management System has one primary focus and that is to increase value for the customer. To achieve this goal you must be able to differentiate between value and non-value (or waste). It is important for employees to develop the ability to clearly define and identify both value and waste:

Value has three elements:

- It is an activity the customer is willing to pay for.

- It transforms the fit, form, or function of a product.

- It is an activity that is done right the first time.

Waste has three elements:

- It is an activity the customer is not willing to pay for.

- It does not transform the fit, form or function of a product

- It is an activity that absorbs resources and increases cost.

Now that you have a clear definition of value and waste from the customer's perspective, it is time to take a step back and look at your business practices in a new light. You need to ask a simple question. Where in your organization are there activities that are not adding value but are using up resources and increasing cost?

Lean principles will guide an organization to take a serious look at the visible causes and effects of waste inside its business processes. Aspects that could get some attention include things like:

(i) inventory

(ii) movement/motion

(iii) waiting or queues

(iv) broken machines or tools

(v) dirt and clutter

(vi) noise

… and many others. We will look into other areas that are creating wasteful practices and driving up costs for the customer.

Chapter 2

Searching for Muda

Many business processes have hidden waste or inefficiencies that we cannot see unless we receive training to demonstrate how to find and recognize them. This is where lean principles can make a difference. It teaches people to see and identify the hidden problems and it teaches them how to use specific tools to find the solutions to correct them.

True to its development and implementation in Japanese organizations, there were many 'legacy' terminologies transferred along with the practices when Western companies started to implement them. There is one terminology that is the most important as we start our discussion about lean tools and their implication for any traditional business.

It is the Japanese term 'muda', which essentially translates into waste (or non-value added activities). In any business process, it is possible to identify one or more of the following eight types of muda or waste, often referred to as the "eight wastes:

1.   Overproduction - making more than the next process can deal with.

2.   Waiting - items, people or equipment sitting idle.

3.   Transportation – moving people, items, or equipment from A to B.

4. Over processing – doing more than is needed to meet the customer's requirements.

5. Excessive inventory – producing more items than the customer order quantity.

6. Defects – not doing it right, first time.

7. Unnecessary motion – additional activities that are unnecessary and increase the processing time.

8. Underutilized people – employees not using their skills or creativity.

There are many reasons why business owners or executive management teams would want to use lean principles in their organization or business. Here are a few examples to demonstrate how lean principles would affect their operations:

(i) Achieve breakthrough performance

(ii) improved quality

(iii) reduce cycle times

(iv) increase value for the customer

(v) stabilizing their business processes throughout every level of the organization

When an organization begins to focus on improving any process, they will have to pay attention to these two statements: *'time is the best measure of effectiveness'*, and *'quality is getting it right, the first time'*. These are two fundamental pillars of lean principles. They will greatly reward an organization that considers them in all aspects of their business practices. To integrate them will require a business to implement the following:

- Grow the capabilities of people by empowering them to improve their own workplace.

- Increase value and achieve cost reductions by identifying and eliminating waste.

- Improve quality by using standard work to focus on *'getting it right, the first time.'*

- Reduce lead/wait times within a short period, in a planned fashion using lean tools to get you there!

- Reduce the processing time from start to finish of the process, i.e. from the moment a customer places an order to when the completed products or services are delivered to the customer.

Lean principles effectively combine and integrate process improvement with business strategy. Next, we will look into how this is achieved.

Chapter 3

Improvement Strategy

There are many different ways to decide which specific approach or improvement projects can have the most impact on a company's bottom line, business strategy and customer satisfaction.

Lean principles are the only fast and easy way to get rid of delays, defects, waiting times, bottlenecks, and unnecessary waste hindering expedient, reliable, efficient and affordable products and services.

A lean philosophy aligned with a practical business strategy is one of the best ways to increase value and customer satisfaction. Waste elimination and cost reduction as a result of using a series of focused improvement events is at the very heart of lean principles and thinking.

The tools and approaches we will be discussing and highlighting as part of this process will be enlightening and inspirational. They are effective and they work. They complement and reinforce the ability to create efficient and effective operations, with measurable returns to the bottom line.

The primary reason for any business to exist at all is to generate revenue and profits. These are the benefits of doing business, otherwise why do it at all? How a company achieves their revenue and profit is a critical factor and will influence how they implement a lean culture. However, the time has passed when business owners could improve productivity by simply asking their employees to roll up their sleeves and work harder. These are the management tools and techniques of the 19th and 20th centuries.

Over the last century many organizations have developed a belief that the best way to eliminate a problem was to throw money at it. Today, most business owners and executive management teams do not have the luxury of being able to throw money at a problem. What they end up with is a bigger problem that is bleeding their profits away. Instead, they must provide the resources to teach their employees to work smarter, not harder!

In a time when producers have to keep up with the constant changing and evolving world, agility and adaptability are the key traits of a successful business. These are only achievable if a company can create an 'organic', collaborative workplace where everyone works together to achieve mutual goals.

Efficient business, transactional, and production practices are an essential part of successful results and outcomes that will serve and enable all of the following:

- There is the definite potential to significantly cut costs, reduce waste, improve productivity, and increase value for the customer. All these can occur at the same time that a business is increasing value, revenues, and profits.

- It is essential to increase awareness in the tools, techniques, and processes necessary to affect these results or outcomes.

- These approaches can help you leverage and position your business to stay ahead of the competition and stand out from the crowd.

Lean principles have helped corporations like GE, Ford, Honda, Nissan and Toyota to lower cost, cut waste, and better utilize their resources, to improve quality, and reduce process time. What is your company leveraging to maintain a competitive edge in the global markets?

If you are paying close attention to process time and quality in your business to increase value for customers, then implementing lean principles is a good choice.

Reducing waiting times, bottlenecks, cycle and lead times all matter to both the business and the customer. Variation in the time it takes to complete any given process (or steps within a process) has to be identified and dealt with to improve quality, cost and delivery. If a company improves these three metrics, they will increase customer satisfaction. This is important because satisfied customers come back with repeat orders time and time again.

To make your operation and business reliable for your customers is the number one priority and this is where lean principles, thinking, approaches, and tools can help.

A business can use specific metrics to determine their performance over a given time period, e.g. monthly, quarterly, annually, etc. These key performance indicators are known as **'QCD'** metrics, which is an acronym for **'Quality, Cost, and Delivery.'**

Quality metrics will measure and track the number of items that are defective to calculate the yield performance to identify how many times a business got it right, first time.

Cost metrics will measure and track activities such as time taken to complete rework or overtime to identify unseen or additional processing costs.

Delivery metrics will measure and track the performance of production velocity (or speed), and if processes are capable of delivering items to the customer on time, every time.

Quality, **C**ost and **D**elivery often suffer in the traditional fast-paced global market, yet the consumer of the 21st century is demanding a successful level in all three as a prerequisite before they will engage in any business transactions. Any business that chooses to ignore this simple fact will do so at its own peril. Any company that decides not to meet these three prerequisites for doing business with consumers will eventually fail and be forced to close its doors.

Traditional companies typically improve at a slow pace. Change requires the desire to become something else and this process takes time. Implementing lean principles will turbo-charge the efforts and give some muscle to the improvement of processes and outcomes. Improved quality, increased speed, and lower cost is what you need and this is why lean principles and thinking are crucial to deliver the best results.

Planning for change requires a strategy that is easy to implement. Keeping it simple is important, so do not make the process more complicated than it needs to be. I developed a model that defines the four phases or steps that a management team must follow when implementing a Lean Management

System. I call the four phase model the *"ISEE Cycle,"* which is an acronym for a continuous cycle of Insight, Strategy, Execute, and Evaluate.

Here is a diagram Fig 1 demonstrating the ISEE Cycle.

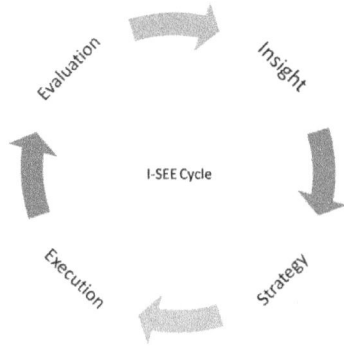

Fig 1: ISEE Cycle – Insight, Strategy, Execute & Evaluate.

I will go through each of the four phases or steps of the ISEE Cycle to give an explanation of their purpose and application as part of a Lean Management System.

Here is a diagram (see Fig 2) showing the linear sequence of events for the four phases or steps of the ISEE Cycle.

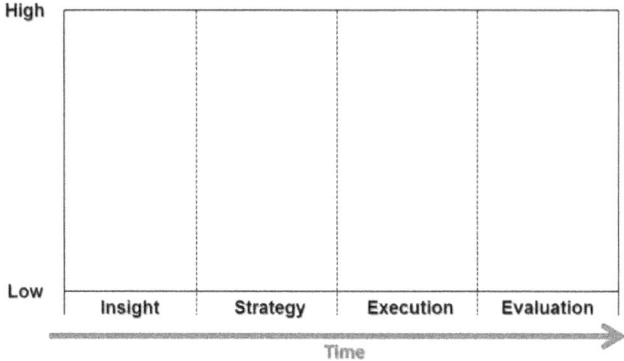

Fig 2: Four phases of the ISEE Cycle

ISEE Cycle Phase 1 - Insight

An organization must be capable of gaining a complete understanding of its strengths and weaknesses. Therefore, the primary focus of the management team's activities during the *Insight* phase of the *ISEE Cycle* is to investigate.

The purpose of the investigation process is to try to understand how a business is currently performing using key performance metrics such as QCD, customer satisfaction, profit, etc. A business owner or management team must be able to identify specific systemic issues that inhibit their organization from delivering value to their customers.

Sadly, for most companies their *Insight* process will be based more on tribal or intrinsic knowledge rather than factual knowledge supported by data. It is this weakness that causes many business owners or managers to be re-active, which forces them to respond in a knee jerk way to problems. *Insight* is the ability to develop and establish a more proactive approach through the use of problem solving techniques.

18

ISEE Cycle Phase 2 - Strategy

When the *Insight* phase is complete, the next step is to define and develop a strategy. The purpose of the *Strategy* phase is to create a detailed plan that will identify and prioritize the strategic initiatives that will determine the improvement of specific business processes.

The reason for focusing valuable resources (e.g. people, time, etc.) on these business processes is because they are responsible for a negative trend in key performance metrics, such as QCD, customer satisfaction, profit, etc. It is important to define an outcome or expected result for each strategic initiative or focused improvement prior to moving into the next phase.

If a management team does not define the expected results, it will create confusion and uncertainty when trying to decide if the strategic initiatives were successfully deployed or not.

ISEE Cycle Phase 3 - Execution

When the *Strategy* phase has been completed, the next step is to implement or execute the strategic initiatives. This is a critical part of the process because an organization must now take their concepts and ideas that are written on flip charts, whiteboards, or paper, and transfer them into the reality of the production floor. This can only be achieved by taking action and executing the strategy or plan. Sadly, it is during this phase of the *ISEE Cycle* where many companies fail miserably. Why is this?

Their failures are the result of committing valuable resources and taking the time and energy to prepare a strategy and then not following through. A plan will only become reality when the actions are implemented. Developing a strategic plan and not following through with it is a total misuse of resources. This is another form of muda or a non-value added activity. Why is this?

An organization removes people from their normal work duties to focus on creating a strategic plan. All their time and effort does not add value until the plan has been successfully executed to deliver the expected results. Here is a diagram Fig 3 that demonstrates the impact of change or improvement during each of the four phases of the *ISEE Cycle*:

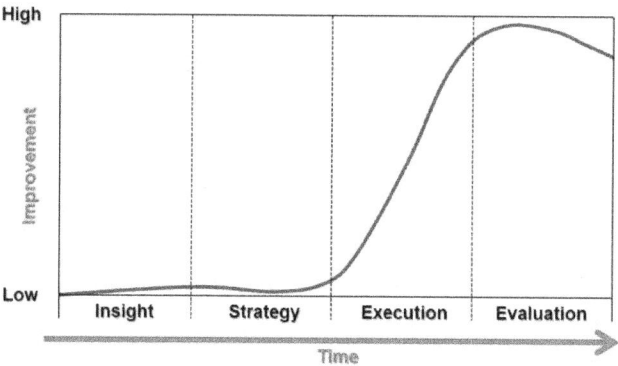

Fig 3: Improvement in phases of the ISEE Cycle.

You can see from this illustration that an organization will not realize the maximum impact of any improvement until it is in the *Execution* phase of the *ISEE Cycle*.

In the next diagram Fig 4, is illustrating the resource requirements during the four phases of the *ISEE Cycle*. You will notice that the resource allocation is high during the

Insight and *Strategy* phases because people are not doing their normal day-to-day work activities. They are focused on defining and developing, identifying and prioritizing the strategic initiatives that will become an integral part of the improvement plan. However, change and improvement does require an investment in time and effort from certain people within the organization to achieve the desired goal.

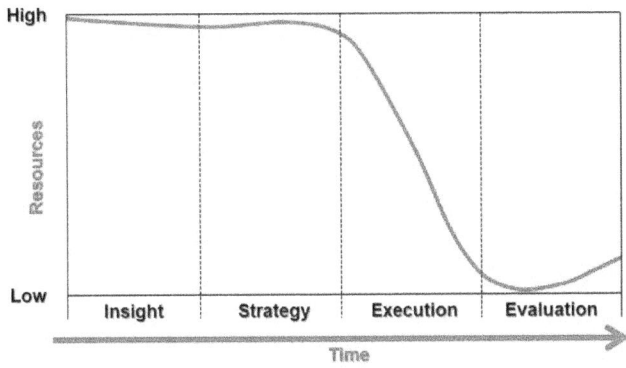

Fig 4: Resource allocation in phases of the ISEE Cycle.

It is important to note in Fig 4 that the resource requirements are lower during the *Execution* and *Evaluation* phases because the managers and employees are performing their normal work duties. This is where they offer the best value for the company and the customer.

When we create an overlay by placing both diagrams from Fig 3 and Fig 4 together, you can see the intersection point of the *Impact* (improvement) line versus the *Effort* (resource allocation) line in Fig 5. The *Effort* line starts at the high point and reduces over time, whereas the *Impact* line starts at the low point and increases over time.

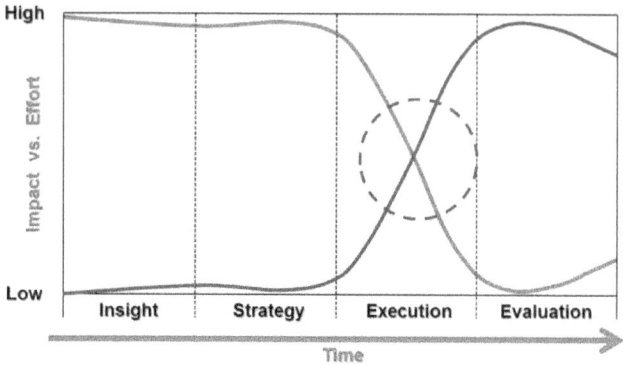

Fig 5: Overlay of Impact vs. Effort.

The area around the intersect point represents the maximum potential for value creation or improvement for the customer. This diagram Fig 5, clearly demonstrates the relationship between the inputs and outputs of business improvement activities. Resource allocation in the *Insight* and *Strategy* phases are non-value added. They do not become value added until they implement the strategic initiatives during the *Execution* phase.

A company that does not use a strategic approach or does not take the time to develop a plan will be continuously re-acting to day to day situations. Their decision making will be the result of a knee jerk response to problems as they fire fight their way from one crisis to the next. I call this type of approach "Chaos Management."

ISEE Cycle Phase 4 - Evaluation

Once the strategic initiatives have been executed the process outputs must be evaluated. This is done by tracking and trending the results to determine if they are in alignment with the expected results defined in the strategic plan.

If the process results are equal to or greater than (≥) the expected results, then the planning procedure during the *Strategy* phase was successful. If the process results are less than (<) the expected results, then the management team will need to identify the root cause using problem solving tools. Once the root cause has been established they will need to define and implement countermeasures to adjust the original plan. This will improve how the strategic initiatives are implemented the next time.

ISEE Cycle - Conclusion

As an organization reaches maturity in their use of the *ISEE Cycle*, the *Insight* phase will change to *Intelligence*. When this occurs, the culture of the organization will shift out of a traditional or re-active business model. The management team will establish a pro-active business system that incorporates problem solving to find solutions.

The *ISEE Cycle* is a recurring and organic process. An organization will go through the cycle over and over again and make adjustments based on real data, not opinions. This will keep the management team focused on implementing the necessary activities to sustain improvements over the long term. An executive management team must understand that to achieve their business goals and objectives, they are going to need to invest some of their valuable resources such as time, effort, people, equipment, etc.

Carpe Diem – Seize the Day!

If you want to develop a sustained value creation and improvement process in your business, then the answer and solution for you is to implement lean principles. Today, you will often find that lean principles are combined with other process and business improvement tools such as Theory of Constraint's, or Six Sigma.

As you start out on this path, it may seem that lean thinking is sometimes counterintuitive. However, it is a brilliant system for yielding great results by applying simplistic methods and the wisdom of many.

A business that embarks on a lean journey will need a team with strong management skills and the ability to lead by example. If you are looking for the one thing that will give any business a competitive edge, this is it! A management team must understand that creating a system that can optimize on the available opportunities for improvement is the name of the game with lean principles.

An organization must quickly learn how to run their processes at a faster pace, while maintaining an acceptable level of quality, lowering cost, and reducing waste. These will reap fast rewards in a short time. However, to take advantage, action is necessary today because the odds are that many of your competitors are also thinking about implementing lean principles.

Many organizations procrastinate and come up with excuses to put off implementing lean principles in the belief that it is necessary to wait for the right moment. What they do not realize is that for every day they wait, they lose the ability to improve their business practices and recover the cost of waste with each day that passes. It is not rocket science, it is simple math. Let me explain. I will use an example of a business that is losing $100 per day because of hidden waste and they wait six months before they decide to implement a lean program. What is the loss in terms of bottom line savings? Here is the math:

First, we need to calculate the number of business days in a six month period. There are 5 business days in a week.

6 months = 26 weeks x 5 business days = 130 days

Potential loss = $100 per day x 130 days = $13,000

Using this example it is easy to realize that the business is losing an opportunity to recover the cost of the waste. This principle applies to every business, no matter what they do or sell. Remember, this was an example but many businesses are losing much more than $100 per day.

You probably have all sorts of questions at this point, like:

- What will lean principles do for any business?
- What is the value proposition for lean principles?
- Why should we do it?
- What happens if we don't do it?

Many have defined lean principles as the streamlining of business processes to get the most out of organizational resources such as equipment, supplies, time, and people.

To keep things simple, lean principles (or a Lean Management System), has a primary goal, which is to *do more with less.*

However, many business owners have misinterpreted this statement. They have separated it into two financial and resource driven outcomes, which are:

a) *'Do the same with less.'*

b) *'Do more with the same.'*

'Do the same with less.' What does this really mean? It means to maintain the current production throughput, while at the same time reducing resources. This approach includes drastic action such as cutting people, budgets, etc.

'Do more with the same.' What does this mean? It means that a business will try to increase production throughput while maintaining the same number or level of resources. This is where they focus on increasing the effectiveness of the business processes to meet customer demand, on-time, every time.

I personally align with the second statement, but not with the first one. Lean principles are not, nor were they ever intended to be used as part of a slash and burn campaign such as reducing headcount, or downsizing a business. If any company chooses to use lean principles in this way, they will destroy any chance of getting their employees to support their continuous process improvement efforts. It will create an environment of fear and distrust. Employees will not willingly participate in, or support a process that puts their jobs and livelihood in danger. Why should they? What is in it for them if they did this?

Achieving the primary goal of lean principles, which is *'doing more with less,'* can be effectively achieved with:

i.   *Less inventory* - Minimizing inventory at all stages of production.
ii.   *Less waste* - Identifying and eliminating hidden waste.
iii. *Less downtime* - Reducing wait times and queues.
iv.   *Less processing time* - Reducing process cycle times between incoming raw materials and finished goods in shipping.

A Lean Management System will create some positive and productive changes in a business that will have a measurable impact on the bottom line.

Here is a list of some of the benefits that a business that implements a Lean Management System could experience:

- Reduced lead time, wait time and cycle time
- Liberated capital
- Increased profit margins
- Increased productivity
- Improved quality
- Just-in-time, affordable, streamlined, cost efficient processes, products and services
- Improved on-time shipments
- Customer satisfaction and loyalty
- Employee retention

As a business- regardless of the scope, range, condition, small, large, start-up, growing or expanding - improvements in quality and time, cost and waste, all matter. A Lean Management System affords a company the opportunity to ensure their business grows stronger, quicker, consistently, with increasing value and improving competitiveness. This will effectively position a business above the masses and mediocrity.

Implementing a Lean Management System is an on-going process. This approach requires a paradigm shift to where the organization is developing the internal discipline to focus on the critical factors. These are reducing time and quality, cost and waste, inventories, work-in-process (often referred to as WIP), floor space, cycle times, and lead times.

Lean principles (even when combined with business improvement efforts such as the Six Sigma methods and discipline), can lead to meaningful and measurable improvements. Most of the lean tools use really simple concepts and are easy to use and implement. They focus on the obvious issues, which are what you can see, change, and control. Lean principles connect the steps, processes, and people. Lean thinking focuses on waste and problems and allows everyone to identify and deal with errors quickly and effectively, while generating savings in the process.

There is nothing really complex or mysterious about it. Every business owner can apply lean principles and implement a Lean Management System into their business, no matter what industry they are in. It does not have to be intricate and only set aside for the chosen few. It can be a great tool to mobilize the creative energy in any organization.

A Lean Management System requires a basic toolkit of lean techniques. These tools will give an organization the capability to identify and improve ineffective processes to where they are operating smoothly. It provides everyone the opportunity to 'take control' and have pride in the work they do. It is a hands-on enabler. When people understand how and what affects processes and their outcomes, they start to visualize the cause-effect relationships happening around them. This level of thinking creates a whole new world of understanding about accountability and how change can occur. It can re-energize a business, and when the rewards start trickling in, everyone partakes and shares in the success and results.

One myth that needs dispelling right off the bat is that a Lean Management System is only for organizations with high sales volume or standardized processes. This is simply misleading and far from the truth. A Lean Management System is versatile and robust enough to be applied to any business process. Whether you are making products, treating patients, or providing a service, a Lean Management System can help in all aspects of doing business, even financial, transactional, and ordering, inventory and HR processes (payroll, hiring etc.).

An executive management team will determine the path for any business. They are responsible for choosing and prioritizing where they will focus the business resources. The executive management team must decide which areas of the business system need improving. A Lean Management System has a series of effective lean tools for helping them to achieve this goal.

Chapter 4

Five Phases to Success

Here are five steps or phases to consider for your business. Each one of these five phases is important if you are contemplating taking a hard look at how you currently operate. The five phases will need to be followed if you are planning to improve your business practices by using lean principles and implementing a Lean Management System:

Phase 1: Leadership and Commitment

Buy-in, championing, and supporting the effort from the top is essential. Decision-makers have to back up what is being planned and visibly support the improvement efforts and projects. Without this support, companies will quickly revert back to old habits and future change will not be possible or feasible.

Vision and direction has to come from the executive or senior management team. They have three key responsibilities to ensure the success of the Lean Management System:

a) Clearly define the goals and expected results for all employees.

b) Provide the resources such as training, equipment, time, etc., so employees are able to achieve the expected results.

c) Remove any barriers that are standing in the way of employees achieving the expected results.

One way of measuring the executive management team's ability to adhere to these three responsibilities is to use key performance metrics that are tracked and trended on performance boards in the work areas. These boards act as a two way communication tool between the management and employees. The performance boards (see Fig 6) clearly define what the management team has planned and expects on a daily basis from the employees in each work area.

Quality		Daily Production Numbers				Value Stream Map
Weekly Monthly		Product	Planned	Actual	Diff +/-	
Cost						5S Information
Weekly Monthly						
Delivery		Problem Solving – A3				Area Layout
Weekly Monthly						

Fig 6: Example of a Performance Board.

At the end of the shift, the employees will have completed their workload for the day and entered the results onto the performance boards. The next step is to compare the actual with the planned or expected result. Is the actual result equal to or greater ($\geq$) than the planned outcome? If not, why are they not the same? If the actual is less than ($<$) the planned outcome there is a place on the performance board for the employees to give feedback to the management team about why they did not achieve the expected result.

The feedback process is not to be used as a big stick to intimidate the employees for failing to achieve the planned or expected numbers. It is to be used to initiate a problem solving process to identify the root cause and find a solution to ensure the employees are able to achieve the expected or planned results in the future. These performance boards demonstrate the management team's commitment to their three core responsibilities, and if they are supporting their employees to achieve the desired results and outcomes.

Phase 2: Educate and Empower:

In this step, an organization must gather the right knowledge and attain the ability to practice lean principles. Training, fundamentals, and even books, consulting, and advice from other businesses that are implementing and experimenting with lean principles can all help you get on your way.

Today, there is no excuse for not giving adequate lean training to employees. There are many companies that can provide online and/or on-site lean training and certification courses at a reasonable price. The one main advantage with online lean training programs is that employees can do this outside of their normal work hours. The online training does not interrupt any production schedules. Many companies are now allowing their employees to stay on after work hours to have access to a computer. Otherwise, they can do the training in the comfort of their own home if they have a laptop or computer and an internet connection. I believe that online training courses are a win-win scenario for the business, the employees, and the customers. Everyone benefits from the increased knowledge and additional skills.

It is a priority to educate and empower, giving people the tools they need. This raises the awareness of lean by introducing and using a couple of the tools at a time over a period of a few weeks or months. The next level is a whole coordinated deployment or roll-out effort with resources and project plans. These are all feasible depending on the needs of the organization and the depth to which they want to integrate the lean principles into their business systems.

Phase 3: Making Waste Visible To All

Understanding processes, cause and effect, root-cause analysis, and even being aware of waste, goes a long way towards discovering and dealing with problems. However, it is important to start small and expand the size of the improvement projects as the company gains more experience. Start by focusing on the low-hanging fruit or easy projects. This will generate an immediate win by demonstrating to the employees how they can see the rewards and experience the benefits right away.

Any improvement that lowers costs is a good thing right? Why not use lean to help you and your employees to SEE and DO something about it. Try to SEE if you can trace the source of waste. DO a 'Waste Walk' by going to the Gemba (or place of work). This is where a team will walk around a facility and try to SEE the 'waste.' The team will identify and document where the waste is occurring. It is also a good idea to carry a digital camera and to take before and after pictures of the work areas.

The team will be searching for evidence of waste, such as discarded items in recycle bins, or defective products, items on the floor, cluttered areas, etc. This can be a great first step. Next, it is important to start to investigate the source of waste and determine how severe the problem is. If possible, start to track the waste by recording the number of scrapped or defective units to determine the actual yield percentage. Any metrics and active tracking heightens awareness of potential problems and their root causes. It allows a team to find creative solutions and to harness the necessary resources to eliminate the waste and save money. All this can happen without an organization having implemented a formal Lean Management System yet! Are you starting to see the potential benefits when using lean principles?

Lean principles are a series of powerful tools and techniques for identifying restrictions in process flow that slow down the production operations, such as bottlenecks, excess inventory, and rework. Getting all the employees involved in these processes gives an organization the opportunity to motivate and mobilize their entire workforce. Imagine if everyone is focused on identifying and eliminating waste with a goal of saving money to increase value for the customer. What kind of change would that create in your business?

Phase 4: Focused Improvement Activities

In this step, an organization will start to map the enterprise level business processes. Identify all the sources of waste and where the business practices are not adding value for the customer. Next, they will make a list and prioritize the areas that need to be focused on and improved in the next twelve months. The easiest way to identify where to start is to ask a simple question: Where are the maximum gains with the minimum effort? Once you identify the area that will give you the *"best bang for the buck,"* observe the processes to get a good understanding of the problem. Collect data, and then analyze it to determine the root cause of the waste.

Next, find a solution to eliminate the root cause and improve the process. Implement the improvements and monitor the new process to ensure that the problem does not reoccur. Track and trend the performance of the improved process to ensure that it stays within the acceptable control limits. It is necessary to develop a plan for sustaining the process over the long term. One method for doing this is to have a project or process champion take the lead and be directly responsible for overseeing the implementation and follow up procedures.

A Lean Management System effectively brings together employees so they can collaborate on each improvement project. A group of motivated people are selected to participate in an improvement event. Many of the team members will be drawn from different departments throughout the organization. There is an important reason for choosing employees from outside of the actual work area that is being observed by the team. The purpose for doing this is to combine their talents and allow them to see the particular issue or topic, area or problem, from several different viewpoints.

Next, define and map the current situation, cost, and waste, to develop a baseline and to diagnose the problem, and set some clear objectives to change and improve the process. These can be metrics or stated SMART (Specific, Measurable, Attainable, Realistic, and Timely) goals, measured in terms of wait or lead-time, process steps, cycle time, floor-space, inventory, and other metrics. An action plan is created and documented to define a list of activities that must be done over a given time-frame as part of the implementation schedule for the improvements. Once the project is completed the group celebrates their successes, outcomes, and results together.

Phase 5: Looking Further Ahead and Beyond

A Lean Management System enables an organization or business to achieve momentum through continued effort and on-going improvement. This is what is referred to in the lean methodology as Kaizen – a Japanese term which loosely translates into the pursuit of continuous improvement.

Now we can take a look at some of the tools and techniques that are integrated into a Lean Management System. We will go through each one to see how they improve and speed up production processes. It is also important to understand how they affect business practices.

Chapter 5

Lean Enterprise Model

The following list of lean tools and techniques are based on the '10 Steps to become a Lean Enterprise' training model that I developed over several years of working with different clients. The model was developed by doing my own research on successful lean implementation projects and trying to determine why the improvement teams achieved such positive results. What I found during my research really surprised me because it was not what I expected. I discovered a common pattern of behavior in the way the teams were being trained and how they used the lean tools during each lean implementation project.

I found that the improvement teams from the most successful projects were trained to use a limited number of lean tools and techniques. In fact, I discovered that it was an average of eleven different lean tools and techniques. This was a big surprise to me because there are literally hundreds of different improvement tools and techniques that are used by companies throughout the world. Was it really this easy? I had to be sure so I decided to formalize the process and I designed and developed the '10 Steps to become a Lean Enterprise' model.

The ten steps are in a specific order, but an organization must only implement steps 1, 2 and 3 in the prescribed sequence. Steps 4 through 9 can be done as and when the resources or opportunities become available. See Fig 7.

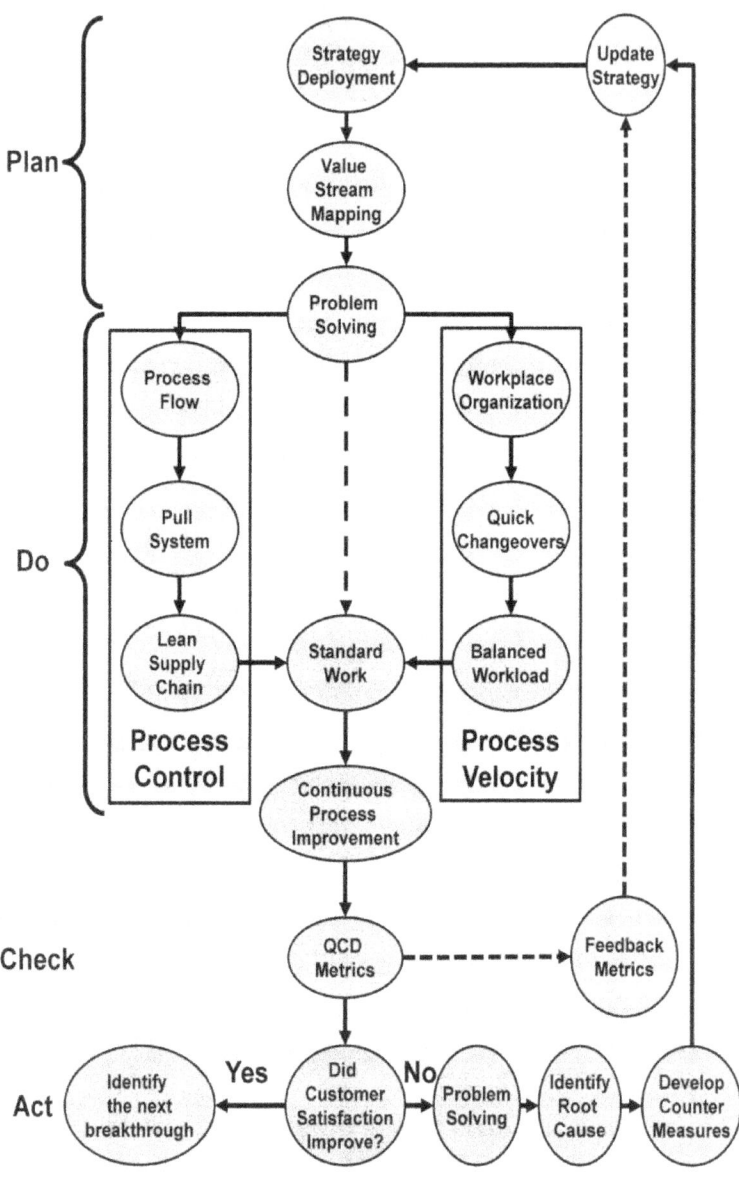

Fig 7: 10 Step Lean Training Model.

Here are the ten steps from the "10 Steps to become a Lean Enterprise" training and implementation model:

Step 1 – Strategy Deployment

Step 2 – Value Stream Mapping

Step 3 – Workplace Organization

Step 4 – Improve Process Flow

Step 5 – Reduce Changeovers

Step 6 – Implement a Pull System

Step 7 – Balance the Workload

Step 8 – Standard Work

Step 9 – Continuous Process Improvement

Step 10 – Lean Supply Chain

In the following chapters of this book, I will go through each of the steps listed in the ten step model.

Chapter 6

Step 1 – Strategy Deployment

Strategy Deployment, (also known as Policy Deployment) was developed in Japan and is known there by the term "Hoshin Kanri." It is a process used to align everyone in an organization with the strategic goals and objectives. A good analogy for Strategy Deployment is to think of it as if a business was planning to go on a journey. What would they need to ensure the successful completion of their journey?

First, they would need to identify where they are going or the final destination – in Strategy Deployment this is called their 'vision.' A vision is a conceptual outline that defines where the company needs to be and what it will look like in the next two to three years.

Next, the company will need to identify their current location – in Strategy Deployment terms this means defining how their business is operating currently. This will require some analysis of financial and operational metrics such as sales, production, costs, etc., to determine how the business has been performing over the last 12 to 24 months.

At this point, the executive management team has two perspectives about the business – a vision which identifies a desired or future state and an assessment of their current state. In other words, they have information about where they want to go, i.e. the final destination, and where they are today, i.e. their current location. The difference between these two location points or states is called the *'strategic gap'* (see Fig 8) and it requires the executive management team to define the course directions and mission to allow them to bridge the gap.

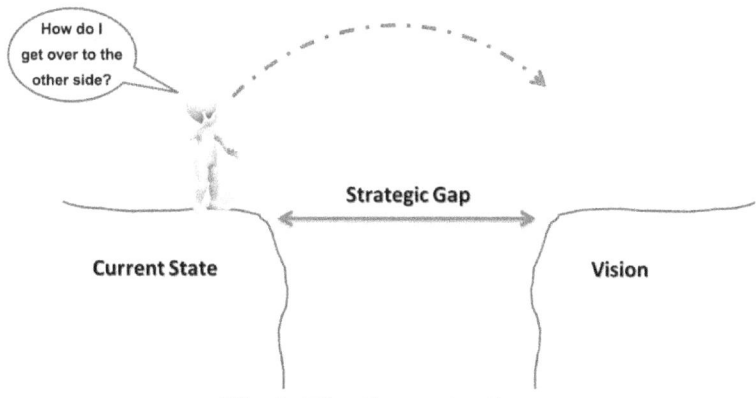

Fig 8: The Strategic Gap.

The next step in the Strategy Deployment process is to define the process that will allow them to embark on the journey to take them from their current state towards their future state or vision. What activities and changes are necessary to make this happen?

These changes and activities are defined as 'breakthrough objectives' (BTO's) and 'annual improvement priorities' (AIP's). They identify the areas of the business that will need to be improved over a two to three year period for the organization to arrive at their future state or final destination. The annual improvement priorities (AIP's) define the three or four specific activities that are required to be completed over the next twelve months to move the organization towards their vision. Both the BTO's and AIP's include clearly defined project milestones for periodic assessments to ensure that the business is on the correct course to reach its final destination or vision.

The vision is often referred to as the 'North Star.' The purpose of Strategy Deployment is to determine what an organization needs to do to align it with its North Star. Action steps such as the BTO's and AIP's are used to align an organization to 'True North' and keep it on course to reach its 'North Star.' I can best demonstrate this process using the "Breakthrough Model' from the book 'Translating Strategy into Action' developed by Duke Corporate Education Inc.

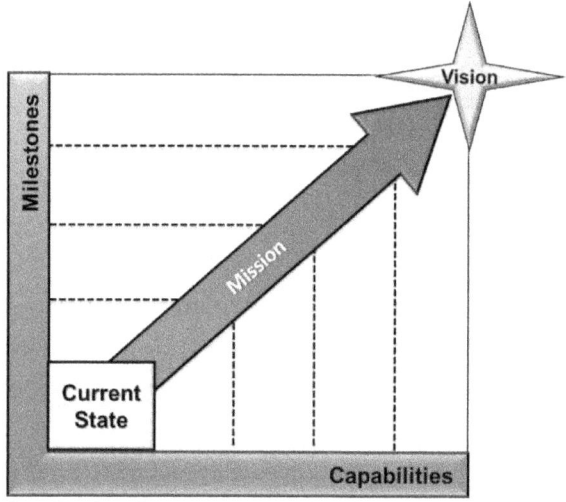

From: Translating Strategy into Action – Duke Corporate Education

Fig 9: Breakthrough Model.

Any business that wants to implement a successful Lean Management System should learn about and implement Strategy Deployment (Hoshin Kanri).

Chapter 7

Step 2 – Value Stream Mapping

In Step 1 – Strategy Deployment, the key areas of the business that needed improving before the business could reach its vision or "North Star" were identified. The process is similar to looking at the organization from an airplane traveling at an altitude of 36,000 feet. You will not see any of the process details from this level, only the outline shape of the buildings.

In Step 2 – Value Stream Mapping, we need to take the airplane down to a lower level to get a more detailed view of the actual processes. At this lower level we will be able to identify and isolate the waste in the system.

Value Stream Mapping has four steps:

1. Collect process data

2. Draw the Current State Map

3. Draw the Future State Map

4. Create an Implementation Plan

We will go through each of these four steps in turn.

Step 1 of 4 - Collect Process Data

An improvement team will observe a process and collect data. They will start from the shipping department and work backwards through the production process until they reach the receiving department. The reason for tracking the production processes in reverse is so the team can see the operations from the perspective of the customer.

The typical data that is collected at each operation will be cycle time, changeover times, quality, and uptime. The team will also document the amount of inventory, the number of employees working at each operation, and the available time per shift or workday.

Step 2 of 4 - Draw the Current State Map

When the team has finished collecting the data, they will organize it into a data set. Next, the team will start to draw a current state map. This is a diagram that shows how the organization receives a customer order and how it activates the process to start to manufacture the product or deliver the service. It includes the information and material flows to demonstrate how the parts are ordered from the suppliers and delivered to the receiving department. All the value and non-value added activities are included in the current state map.

When the team has finished drawing the current state map, they will start to identify the waste using an icon called a "Kaizen Burst."

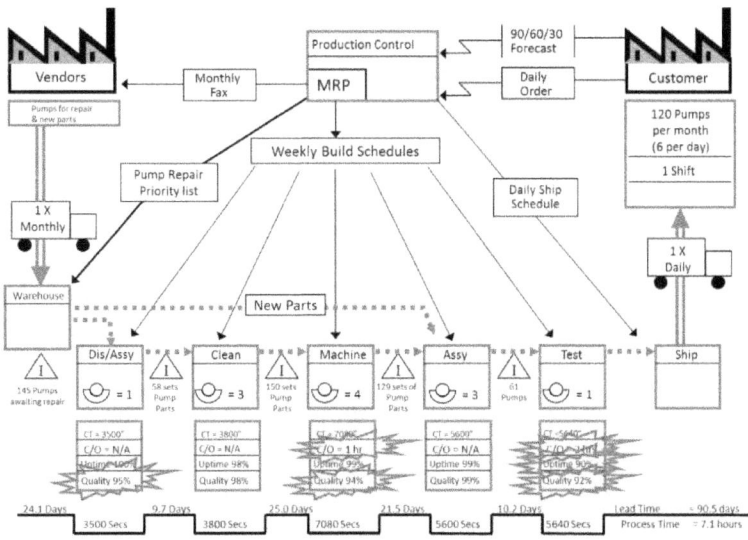

Fig 10: Example of a Current State Map.

In the diagram (see Fig 10) you can see an example of a current state map. The team will look for specific locations where there are imbalances in the process creating delays, defects, or excessive inventory. Remember, they are only looking for the waste. The team is not ready to find solutions to fix the problems. This will happen when they start to draw the future state map.

Step 3 of 4 - Draw the Future State Map

The team will use the current state map to identify which locations or areas are going to give the best bang for the buck. This is how they will prioritize what to change and when to change it. This is a critical element in the improvement process because any business owner or management team wants to use their available resources in the most productive and cost effective manner. The goal is to identify and eliminate waste in order to improve quality and delivery to reduce cost.

An improvement process requires employees to be taken away from their normal work duties to be part of an improvement team. This means that while they are away from their job they are not producing what the customer wants. Therefore, it is important to know that their time is well spent and focused on something that will eliminate waste and improve value for the customer. If the improvement team member's time is not being utilized effectively, then this is simply another form of waste (or muda).

Next, they will try to find solutions to eliminate the waste and improve the information and materials flows. The team will go through the exercise of eliminating the waste to create the future state map. Once completed, the future state map is an improved version of the current state map but with the waste removed. You can see this reflected in the timeline in the diagram of a future state value stream map (see Fig 11).

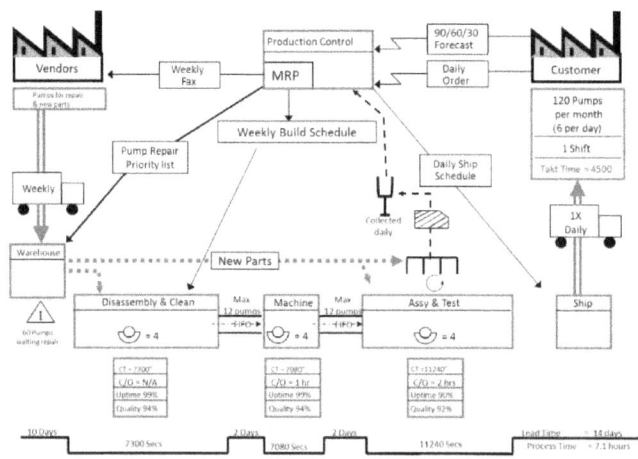

Fig 11: Example of a Future State Map.

46

Compare the sample current state map with the future state map and you will see that the total lead time for the process was reduced from 90.5 days to 14 days. This was achieved without moving any equipment, or interruption to the production schedule. However, it is important to note that everything to this point has been done on paper and nothing has been implemented.

Step 4 of 4 - Implementation Plan

The next step is to get the organization to implement the changes identified in the future state map. To do this they will have to create an implementation plan. This is a detailed action plan showing how the business processes will change from the current state into the future state. It will be necessary to clearly define the Who, What, Where, When, Why, and How (5W+1H) for each of the activities.

The implementation activities will need to follow a 'critical path' to ensure that the improvements are implemented in the correct sequence. As each action item is implemented, it is important to make sure the employees in the work area receive training to let them know how to use the new process and to understand the expected results. The management and improvement team will start to observe and monitor the new process for a short period to see if it is performing correctly. If is not, they will make minor adjustments to the process as and when they are needed.

In diagram Fig 12, you can see an example of a Value Stream Mapping Implementation Plan.

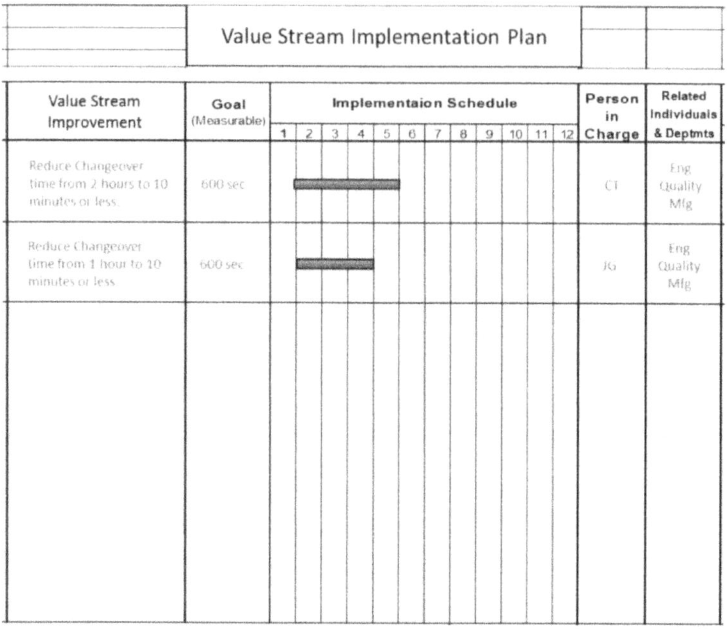

Value Stream Improvement	Goal (Measurable)	Implementaion Schedule												Person in Charge	Related Individuals & Deptmts
		1	2	3	4	5	6	7	8	9	10	11	12		
Reduce Changeover time from 2 hours to 10 minutes or less	600 sec		▦▦▦												CT	Eng Quality Mfg
Reduce Changeover time from 1 hour to 10 minutes or less	600 sec		▦▦▦												JG	Eng Quality Mfg

Value Stream Implementation Plan

Fig 12: Value Stream Mapping Implementation Plan.

The key question that I always get asked is "When is the Value Stream Mapping exercise complete?"

The answer to this question is easy: "When the future state becomes the current state!" Then you start the same process over again because business systems and customer demand are constantly changing.

Chapter 8

Step 3 – Workplace Organization

Workplace Organization is a fundamental tool in a Lean Management System. It contains two elements, which are 5S and Visual Management. 5S can help any business to adopt a disciplined approach for re-organizing the workplace to get rid of clutter and waste. Visual Management can help to create a visual workplace and make it easy to differentiate between a normal and abnormal situation at a glance.

Five S's (5S)

Cleanliness and having a set place for everything is the key to the successful transition of any business into a Lean Enterprise. The mantra for a 5S system is "A place for everything and everything in its place." If a company cannot implement a robust 5S process, they do not have the level of internal discipline to become a Lean Enterprise. 5S creates a solid foundation. Without it, the lean infrastructure is like that of a house built on sand. Over time it will fall apart and disappear.

The name for the 5S system stems from the Japanese words that have been translated into English meanings and equivalent words for…

1. Sort (Seiri)
   - Separate necessary from unnecessary items
2. Set in Order (Seiton)
   - Create a defined location for necessary items

3. Shine (Seiso)
   - Cleaning, inspection and daily maintenance
4. Standardize (Seiketsu)
   - Develop a standard procedure for first 3S's
5. Sustain (Shitsuke)
   - Ensure the 5S process is a daily habit

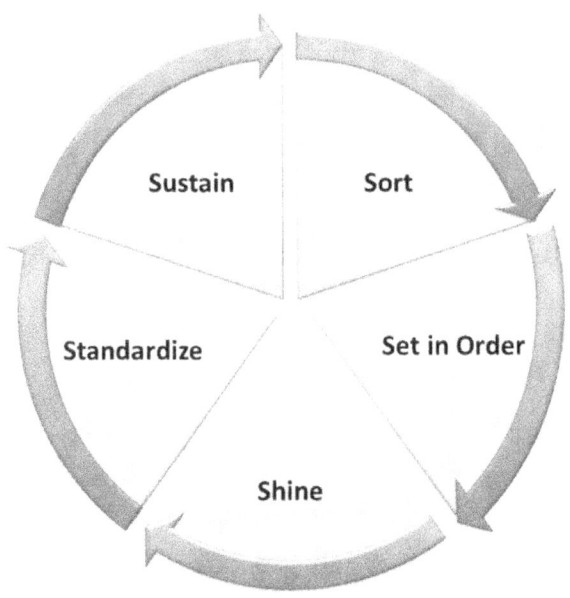

Fig 13: 5S System.

The purpose of 5S is to help a business to reduce costs by eliminating waste. The main type of waste that is eliminated is the time needed for employees to go searching for materials, equipment, information, supervision, etc. When an employee is searching for any of these items they are not being productive. In fact, production is probably at a standstill while they are away from their work area.

Many companies are now implementing a 6S system, which is also known as "5S+1." It includes the same five activities as the standard 5S system but with an additional 'S' for Safety. Many lean purists see this as unnecessary or overkill because they consider safe practices to be inferred in the original version of the 5S system developed by Taiichi Ohno at Toyota. Some companies have gone even further and have included other elements into their workplace organization systems such as adding an 'S' for Security.

The number of S's is not really the problem as far as 5S or 6S is concerned. This is simply another distraction that draws people away from the core issue. I fully understand that an important part of progress is to innovate, improve, and adapt systems to meet the needs of modern business environments. This is the very nature of continuous process improvement (or Kaizen).

The more important issue is the development of an infrastructure and the discipline to support the application and sustainment of a viable system. So, the number of S's is not the point of the exercise. It is the ability to demonstrate through objective evidence that a business is capable of implementing and maintaining a clean and organized workplace. Seeing 5S in practice is what makes people believe in the process, by demonstrating that it actually works and improves their environment!

Visual Management

Visual Management is creating a visual workplace where it is easy to immediately recognize when something is not how it should be or in its designated location. It incorporates signs, lines, and labels to identify things. One common method is the use of color coding and visual cues to know when something is missing or out of place.

A good example of visual management is designating color codes for different work areas. A small dab of paint or piece of electrical tape is placed on the equipment and tooling in each area. If tools with red paint or tape appear in the green work area then you know at a glance that they are in the wrong place and need to be returned to their designated location. If this problem persists and the wrong color coded tooling is consistently appearing in another work area, then it is an indication of a problem. The work area that keeps borrowing the tooling does not have their own. It would be necessary to purchase another set of tooling to stop them removing it from the other work area.

CAN-DO

Another tool that can help to direct your focus in the area of workplace organization and add a motivational element to a Lean Management System is the "CAN-DO" process.
Following this simple process will set an organization on the right track towards becoming a Lean Enterprise.

CAN-DO STEPS:

1. C - Cleanup
2. A - Arranging
3. N - Neatness
4. D - Discipline
5. O - Ongoing improvement

It is important to define each of the steps in the CAN-DO process. For example:

1. What is your definition of cleanup for a work area?
2. What is your definition of arranging a work area?
3. What is your definition of neatness in a work area?
4. How will you maintain the discipline?
5. How are you going to identify ongoing process improvements in the work area?

Employees will need to know and understand the answers to these questions. If not clearly defined there will be no standard established for them to know what is expected of them.

Chapter 9

Step 4 – Improve Process Flow

One of the most effective measures of competitiveness is the amount of time it takes a business to turnaround an order to deliver the products to the customer. This total time is called "lead time." There are many issues that have a direct impact of process lead time, and the most common are "bottlenecks" throughout the production processes. These bottlenecks restrict the flow of raw materials and information, parts and people, which slows down the manufacturing process (see Fig 14).

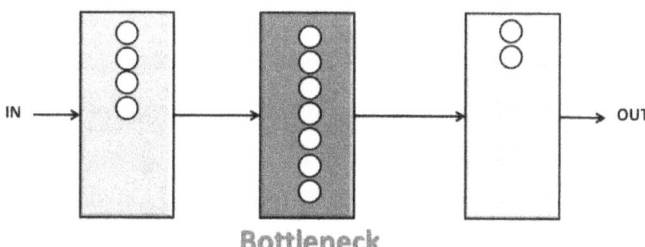

Bottleneck

Fig 14: It is easy to identify a bottleneck as items start to back up at the 2nd operation.

First, we need to define "Process Flow." It is the movement of information and materials through a manufacturing process using the most effective methods. What are the most effective methods?

The most effective method for improving process flow is to implement Step 3 - Workplace Organization (using 5S and visual management techniques). The next important method will be to improve the actual design of the work area. A well designed work area will allow components, information, and people, to flow in and out without any restrictions. At the point where a process has a restriction to flow, it causes items to back up behind it. The location where these items are starting to pile up in the production process is called "a bottleneck or a constraint."

The purpose of Step 4 - Improve Process Flow, is to understand what causes bottlenecks and how to reduce or eliminate them. This will require an improvement team to observe, document, and analyze two sectors of the work area:

1. The actual design of the workstation to understand how an employee is physically performing their tasks to manufacture the products.

2. The layout of the work area around the workstation to determine how it influences the flow of materials, parts, people, equipment, etc., in and out of the work area

Both of these elements affect process flow in a manufacturing facility. An improvement team will need to focus on both to effectively change a process.

In Step 3 - Workplace Organization, the work areas were reorganized and the necessary items placed into designated locations. The next step is to try to improve the way that the work is moving in and out of the work areas. One method for doing this is using a "cellular layout." This is where the work areas are converted into cells which have designated areas for certain activities. The reason for using a cellular layout is to minimize the movement of people and equipment, materials and products. It will improve the flow to and from the cell, which will speed up the production process, therefore reducing lead times.

The most effective layout design for a cellular layout is called a "U shaped cell," see Fig 15. It is an effective layout that is utilized by organizations that are implementing lean principles. Why is this? It is because it has the smallest footprint and uses less floor space. The "U shaped cell" allows the most efficient movement of people, materials, parts, and information from operation to operation.

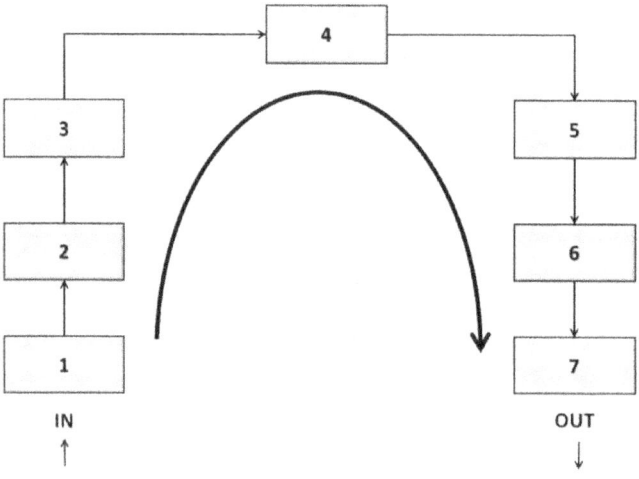

Fig 15: U shaped cell design.

What Happens to a Product?

When we start to study the process flow, we can identify three specific occurrences that are consistently repeated during the sequence of events. In each moment as it transits through the production process, a product can and will be experiencing any one of these three situations:

1. It is waiting

2. It is being moved

3. It is being processed

Which of these three situations are creating value for the customer versus non-value (or waste)?

1. It is waiting   = *Waste, increases cost*

2. It is being moved   = *Waste, increases cost*

3. It is being processed   = *Adding value for the customer*

Where would you start to focus your valuable business resources to improve the process flow?

If you said "To identify the root causes of waiting" you are correct. Products tend to spend too much time being inactive or sitting idle waiting for something to happen. It is important to determine the reasons for the waiting time.

Here are some examples to demonstrate why the products are waiting:

- Waiting because an employee is searching for equipment.
- Waiting because an employee is searching for information.

- Waiting because an employee is searching for materials.
- Waiting for the machine to be set-up.
- Waiting for the next available machine.
- Waiting for the next available person.
- Waiting for input from another department.
- Waiting for parts to be delivered.

Any one of these situations is adding cost because it is increasing the amount of time it takes for a product to pass through the entire production system.

The same method can be applied to determine when and why a product is being moved. It is unrealistic to believe that you will be able to eliminate all the movements of a product. However, the purpose of the exercise is to improve the process by identifying and eliminating any unnecessary movements of products, materials, parts, information, or people. Here are some examples to demonstrate why the products are being moved:

- Moved aside to make way for something else.
- Moved to another department.
- Moved onto a machine.
- Moved off a machine.
- Moved into storage.
- Moved out of storage.
- Moved for no reason.
- Moved for a good reason.

Identifying and eliminating the root causes of waiting and moving should be the primary focus of your Lean Management System. The only part of the process flow that adds value for the customer is when the product is being processed. How do we define the activities when a product is being processed?

A product is being processed when it is being transformed to meet the customer's specifications or requirements. Here are some examples of a product being processed:

- A product is being painted.
- A product is being machined.
- A product is being assembled.
- A product is being dis-assembled.
- A product is being shot blasted.
- A product is being labeled

So, remember that an easy way to improve process flow is to focus on the reason why products, parts, materials, and people are waiting, or are being moved.

Chapter 10

Step 5 – Reduce Changeovers

Customers want to purchase products when they need them. Most companies make some of their customers wait because they have to schedule their resources to try to meet the demands of their customers. One of the major issues in a traditional production system is their inability to easily transition from manufacturing one product and changing over to the next product. This creates lots of waste in the form of lost production hours because of process downtime and leads to a company holding excessive inventory levels.

Also, the machine is sitting idle. It cannot produce anything while it is being set-up. A business must find a way to reduce their changeover times to increase the flexibility of their production system. If they can achieve this they will be able to make what the customer wants, when they need it. This will increase value for the customer and reduce costs for the company.

A traditional changeover begins when the machine stops because it has finished producing a part. With the production run complete and the machine available for changeover, a traditional set-up team will start to gather their equipment, tools, materials, etc. The machine will sit idle until it can be set-up to run the next scheduled part and it can start production again. Every hour of downtime due to a changeover is one hour of lost production time. How can an organization reduce the downtime for changeovers to increase their available production hours?

They have to start by understanding the definition of a changeover. The correct definition of a changeover is:

"The time period between the last good item off the current production run and the first good item off the next production run."

It is very important to clearly understand this definition of a changeover. It is the first step towards identifying, measuring, and tracking machine downtime as a consequence of changeovers. The total changeover time period breaks down into four separate elements:

1. Preparation.
2. Removal and replacement.
3. Measurement and calibration.
4. Trial runs and minor adjustments.

Here is a pie chart that includes the percentage of time for each of these four elements.

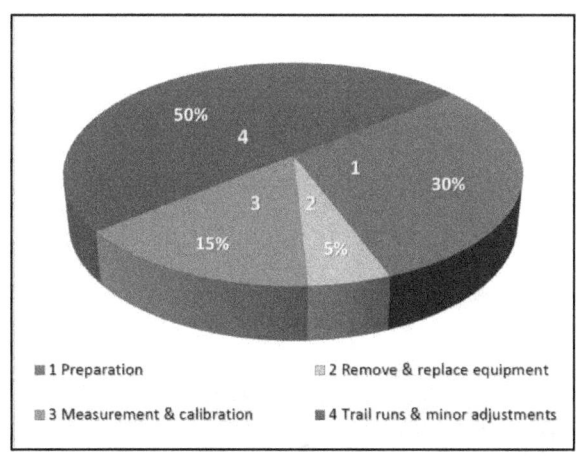

Fig 16: Pie Chart of Changeover Elements.

What is astonishing is that the fourth element of "Trial runs and minor adjustments" takes as much as 50% of the total changeover time.

The next is "Preparation" with 30%, and then "Measurement and calibration" with 15% of the total changeover time. "Removal and replacement," which most people think of as the actual changeover process, only actually takes 5% of the total time.

In reality, there are several things happening during the changeover time. To identify each of these activities, we will use a process called "**SMED**." This is an acronym for "**S**ingle **M**inute **E**xchange of **D**ie." It is a system developed by Shigeo Shingo to reduce equipment changeover times in a manufacturing environment.

The SMED system involves four steps to reduce changeover times. An improvement team will need to follow these four steps in the prescribed order to get the best results.

The four steps for reducing changeovers are:

1. Document and record a changeover.
2. Separate activities into internal and external elements.
3. Convert internal elements into external elements.
4. Streamline all aspects of the changeover process.

Each of these steps is a critical element in reducing changeovers and increasing the scheduling flexibility throughout the production process.

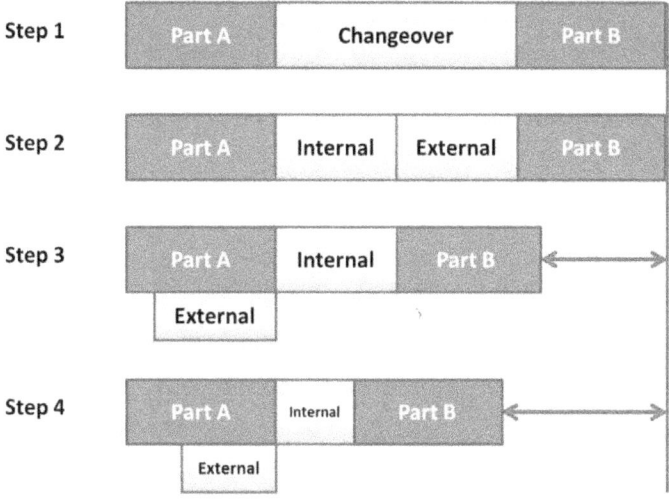

Fig 17: The Four Steps of SMED.

Each of the four steps is a natural progression through the process of improving a changeover. In other words, the completion of one step creates the opportunity to move into the next step in the sequence.

In Step 2, the changeover activities are separated into internal and external elements. An internal element is an activity that can only be performed when the equipment is stopped. An external element is an activity that can be performed at any time. However, the preference is for it to occur while the machine is still running and producing parts.

In Step 3, the improvement team will re-organize the changeover activities to try to get all the external activities to occur while the machine is still running and producing. This will significantly reduce the amount of downtime.

63

Chapter 11

Step 6 – Implement a Pull System

One of the most common forms of waste in a traditional business is the amount of time an item sits waiting for the next process to become available. This has a direct impact on the movement of items, people, information, etc. This causes the production system to experience a consistent series of interruptions, which will force it to slow down, stop, and start up again and again. A business must find a better way to control its production system to try to eliminate these interruptions to process flow.

We need to start by first defining a "Pull system." It is a method of activating a production system after a customer consumes a specific product or service. In other words, when a customer purchases an item it creates an empty space in the finished goods area. This empty space is a visual cue that sends a signal back through the production process to replenish the empty space with another product. Pull Systems work well with "Make to Order" or "Make to Stock" businesses.

You will see the same process when you walk into the supermarket to buy bread, and you pay for the bread at the checkout counter. The transaction sends a signal back to the person who is responsible for ordering the bread, telling them to buy more to replenish the shelves. In turn, they contact the bread company and purchase more bread. The bakery will bake and package the bread. They deliver the bread, and very often their own employee who is driving the delivery van will replenish the bread on the shelves at the supermarket.

Taiichi Ohno got the idea for the "Pull System" after a visit to the USA. While there, he went into a supermarket and observed an employee replenishing goods on the shelves.

He implemented the pull system at Toyota, and it became an integral part of the Toyota Production System (TPS).

Most companies will experience problems when trying to make the transition from batch and queue manufacturing processes to implement single piece or continuous flow (see Fig 18).

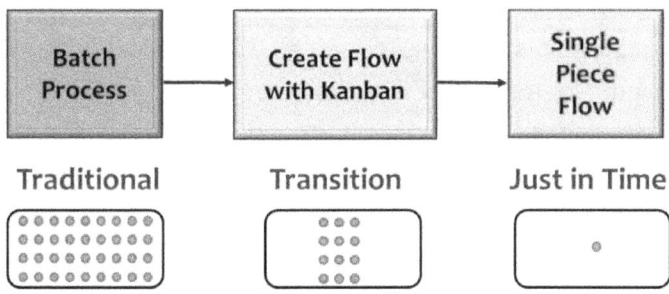

Fig 18: Transition from Batch to Single Piece Flow.

To help them to smooth out some of the issues as they work through the transition process they will use something that is called "Kanban." This is a Japanese term that means 'card or signal.'

Kanban is often referred to as an intelligent buffer because it is used to create a visual inventory control method. It can be in the form of a card, flashing light, audible sound, lines on the floor creating a rectangle or circle, or any other visual indicator to relay the necessary replenishment information.

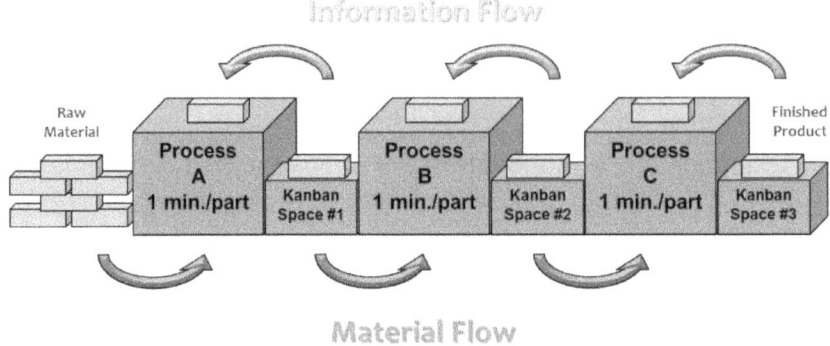

Fig 19: Example of Kanban being used to link processes.

Kanban integrates what has come to be known as the three C's: Command, Control, and Communicate:

1. It visually commands which item needs to be replenished next by having the necessary customer order information at the point of use.

2. It visually controls the inventory to a pre-determined maximum quantity, which is clearly defined on the Kanban card or supporting documentation.

3. It visually communicates when an item needs to be replenished by establishing pre-defined replenishment limits to be able to meet customer demand (takt time).

The item description, re-order quantity, supplier, etc., is usually identified on the Kanban card or supporting documentation. You can see an example of a Kanban card with some of these details in Fig 20.

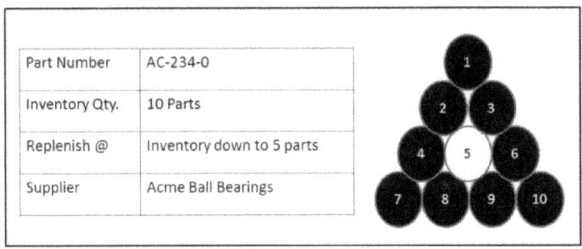

Part Number	AC-234-0
Inventory Qty.	10 Parts
Replenish @	Inventory down to 5 parts
Supplier	Acme Ball Bearings

Fig 20: Example with product details on Kanban card.

Some companies will never be capable of achieving a true single piece or continuous flow manufacturing process. They will implement a Pull System that will link their processes using Kanban to follow the principles defined in the 3C's: Command, Control, and Communicate.

The use of Kanban will help them to keep a tighter grip on the amount of inventory at each process. The pre-defined amount of inventory is called 'Standard Work in Process (SWIP).'

Chapter 12

Step 7 – Balance the Workload

In lean manufacturing circles most people think of the Japanese term "muda" as a generic word for waste. Every organization that is implementing lean principles will focus their resources on the identification and elimination of muda. However, there are two other aspects of waste that most people don't often talk about. These are also Japanese's terms, and they are called "muri (overburden)" and "mura (unevenness)." It is necessary to reduce both muri and mura to try to balance a production system and improve process flow.

To balance the workload, an organization has to study two key elements of production which are:

1. Work Content

2. Work Scheduling

Work Content: Is the total time required for an employee to perform a series of specific activities to complete one item before they can pass it onto the next process. It is represented as the cycle time per part, i.e. the number of seconds, minutes, etc., to complete one assembly.

Work Scheduling: Is timing the delivery of parts, materials, and/or sub-assemblies to allow an employee to complete their work content. These are delivered at a specific pace so an employee can complete their work tasks in a timely manner to meet a customer order delivery date.

Imbalances in the work content and scheduling are major causes of bottlenecks. It is the same as too many automobiles on a freeway. The constraint will slow traffic to a crawl and cause it to back up for miles. The traffic will move slowly, then stop and start up again. The flow will be erratic and inconsistent. In Fig 21 you can see an example of a cycle time analysis chart demonstrating a series of operations that have imbalanced cycle times (or work content). The bottleneck is the machining process because it has the longest cycle time (in seconds).

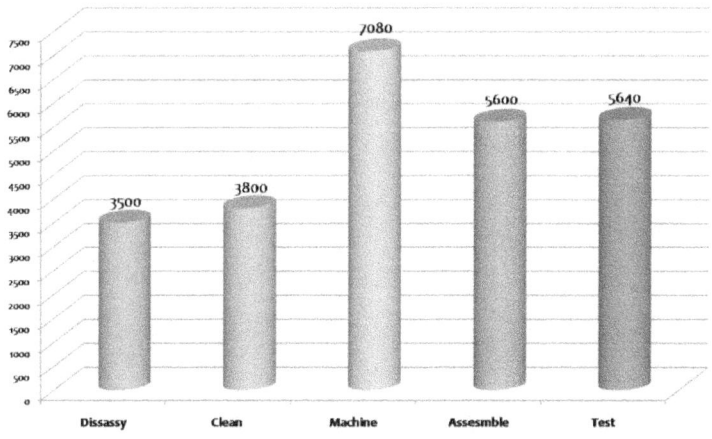

Fig 21: Example of a Cycle Time Analysis Chart.

There are several ways that constraints can manifest:

1. Taking too much time to complete a task will slow down the production system.

69

2. Manufacturing too many parts will eventually overwhelm the process.

3. Not producing enough parts will create erratic activity along a production line with processes repeatedly stopping and starting.

4. Not enough people working in the production system will eventually cause employees to become overwhelmed and can lead to quality problems.

5. Inconsistent flow of customer orders through the production system.

It is important to find ways to balance the work content and work scheduling to increase confidence in an organization's capability to consistently meet customer demand.

Chapter 13

Step 8 – Standard Work

In a traditional company, employees often develop their own practices as they learn how to do their jobs. A company that is implementing a Lean Management System is trying to develop a consistent and repeatable method to help identify and eliminate waste.

The best way to create this level of consistency is to take the best practices and document them so every employee can be trained to perform their job to deliver the best results. One of the main benefits of identifying these best practices and documenting them is an improvement in product quality.

All employees who perform a particular operation are encouraged to use the standard work to ensure they are completing their tasks in alignment with the documented method. It is preferable to make these documents visual by using pictures or drawings to depict the methods or processes.

The purpose for establishing standard work is to create a repeatable and consistent methodology to stabilize the process, to improve the quality, and to reduce process variation. A standard work document will define the number of people, work activities, and resources, required to complete a process.

A standard work document is an excellent tool for training new employees or maintaining the standards of current workers. In many cases, standard work will identify and document existing waste or non-value added activities.

When any process is improved, the standard work document is updated to reflect the new method, and it is used to train the current workforce to follow the new standard process.

Chapter 14

Step 9 – Continuous Improvement

The one trait that separates a business that successfully implements a Lean Management System from one that fails is the way they see and deal with problems.

A successful business will see a problem as an 'opportunity for improvement.' They will use problem solving tools to find a solution to eliminate the root cause of the problem. On the other hand, an unsuccessful company will see problems as a necessary evil and something they have to put up with if they want to be in business.

Continuous Process Improvement (CPI) is achieved by identifying problems and finding solutions. Therefore, problem solving tools and techniques are an important part of a Lean Management System.

A3 – A Problem Solving Storyboard

An A3 got its name from the metric size of the sheet of paper that was used to create it at Toyota in Japan. In the U.S.A, an 11" x 17" sheet of paper is the nearest size to A3.

An A3 uses an eight step model that follows a logical process to define, analyze, improve, and eliminate the root cause(s) of a problem. Incorporated into the eight step process is PDCA – Plan, Do, Check, and Act (also known as the Deming Cycle). See an example of an A3 template in Fig 22.

The eight steps included in an A3 process are:

Step 1 – Define the problem (PLAN)

Step 2 – Understand the current condition (PLAN)

Step 3 – Define the target condition (PLAN)

Step 4 – Analyze the data (Root Cause Analysis) (PLAN)

Step 5 – Define the countermeasures (PLAN)

Step 6 – Develop an implementation plan (DO)

Step 7 – Evaluate the improvements (CHECK)

Step 8 –Follow up to sustain the improvements (ACT)

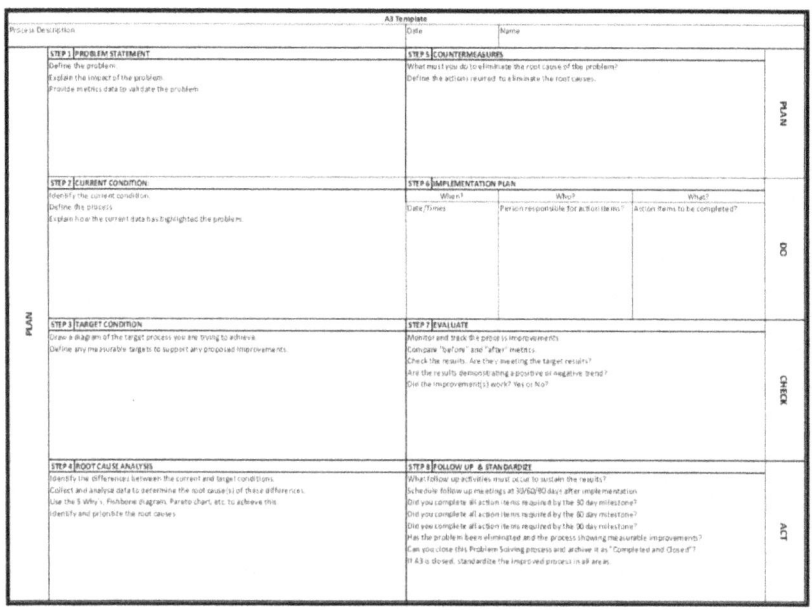

Fig 22: An example of an A3 Template.

An A3 is a powerful CPI tool and is used by every Lean Enterprise as an integral part of their Lean Management System to document their problem solving projects. It helps everyone to stay focused and to clearly understand the actions and sequence of events that are necessary to identify and eliminate the root cause of a problem.

Mistake-proofing (Poka-Yoke)

The goal of a Lean Management System is to eliminate waste and defects that are a major contributor to increasing costs because of ineffective processes and quality. To achieve this goal, an organization must be able to transition from a reactive to a more proactive approach. One lean methodology that helps a business to focus on this transition is error or mistake proofing, which is a translation of the Japanese term "Poke Yoke."

Mistake proofing is a system that uses built-in safeguards and reduces defects to zero. It highlights problems as they occur. This is a critical factor in not letting mistakes, oversights, and errors slip through to reach the customer. Processes are designed around this principle to be more efficient, and will help your business eliminate waste by reducing the costs of defects and rework. Mistake-proofing is important part of the TPM process. It will help to reduce variability, while increasing process capability.

Total Productive Maintenance (TPM)

Yet another essential Lean Management System tool and utility to consider is something referred to as Total Productive

Maintenance (TPM). This is different from routine or occasional maintenance that has to be performed. Having no downtime and scheduled maintenance as a result of pro-active planning, as opposed to a more re-active approach is recommended in the Lean Management System philosophy and its practical application.

TPM is often depicted as "deterioration prevention." It is not focused on fixing machines when they break down. There is much more involved in the TPM process. Equipment must be ready at any and all times to meet operational needs. The equipment should be able to provide efficiency on demand, while running and providing a quality service and output.

Overall Equipment Effectiveness (OEE)

OEE uses three key performance metrics: quality, availability (or uptime), and throughput, to track the performance of the equipment. OEE will gage how the maintenance tasks are meeting the demands of the manufacturing processes. It will give valuable feedback about what should be done, when it should be done, and who should do it to keep the equipment working continuously to meet customer demand.

Chapter 15

Step 10 – Lean Supply Chain

Every business has two critical factors that must be considered during their lean implementation process. These are customers and suppliers. Without both of these, a company will fail to establish market share and sustain itself.

Many traditional organizations do not work to develop collaborative relationships with their suppliers. They often choose their suppliers based on the lowest price. However, many learn the hard way because if their suppliers fail to meet their needs, the organization will fail to meet their own customer's needs.

In Step 10, an organization has to widen their focus from their own internal processes to include their external supplier and customer processes. They will have made some improvements in Step 6 – Implement a Pull System. The business could have connected their pull system using Kanban in their customer's receiving department and inventory system.

Lean Supply Chain is a complex subject in itself. It is outside the scope of this publication because it would take an entire book to cover the procedures for developing a lean supply chain.

Chapter 16

Competitive Advantage

You cannot change what you do not acknowledge or know about. Lean principles bring an awareness to 'take note' and observe your environment (cost, waste, movement, clutter, scrap, etc.) and then **DO** something real, meaningful, and constructive about it!

What improvements should and could be made are both important questions to ask, prioritize, and act upon.

Issues such as lead time, waiting and cycle time, quality, cost and inventory; in fact anything that affects the customer, should be dealt with expediently. Focus on the processes that are defined as "internal and controllable." There is no point trying to change things that you do not have direct control over when starting out.

Asking the right type of questions could provide you with hints as to a strategy, starting point, and priority for action:

- Which process or step should get immediate attention – where is the biggest WIN-WIN for both the customer and the company?

- What are all the priorities that we need to pay attention to in this organization/business and operation? Map the processes and make the list. Then ask in what order you should tackle the priorities?

- How do we get the best improvements the quickest way? How does an organization tap into the benefits of a Lean Management System right away?

If reducing overhead, quality costs, and inventory to save money and become a streamlined and cost-efficient provider are keys to your business success, a Lean Management System can help your business in all aspects and areas.

Taking the theory of a Lean Management System to the practical implementation will take planning, patience, and persistence. It will also require determination, detail, and discipline. These are often referred to these as the Three P's and the Three D's to make them easy to remember. Gradual, planned, focused effort is what it is all about. Step-by-step instructions and actions to deliver improvements over time that can be sustained in a stable and predictable way are essential.

If any of the following scenarios are important to your business, a Lean Management System can help you reach the defined targets and goals for management, employees, and customers:

- Increasing operating margin and revenue
- Reduce manufacturing lead, wait, and cycle times
- Reduce costs with less WIP or work-in-progress inventory (half completed products). Time and space costs money!
- Reducing manufacturing overhead and quality costs
- Increase gross profit margin

- Get customers what they want, when they want it, anytime, every time, and all the time - quickly and correctly, affordably, and on-demand.

- Achieve consistent quality and low defect rates (scrap/waste)

Improve the performance of the value streams and an organization cannot go wrong, they can only get better. They will achieve improvements and higher levels of quality to increase customer satisfaction and reduce costs to remain competitive and profitable.

Keep business processes under control and continue to improve every day, and this will position the company head-and-shoulders above the masses. The management team must define and execute a well-planned and gradual deployment of a Lean Management System throughout the organization to achieve the desired outcomes, results, and success!

One of the best methods for having a measurable impact resulting in dramatic improvements in any business is reading and listening to customer complaints. Many companies see customer complaints as a bad thing, but these can give invaluable feedback to identify where some of the major problems might lie within specific business processes. However, it requires an organization to be honest and open about their internal business practices and how they affect their customers. An organization should never hesitate to ask their customers for feedback! Customers will tell it like it is. It is also a wonderful opportunity to let customers know that what they want, say, and need really matters. An organization that is capable of providing this kind of responsive and personalized service will secure a loyal customer base today and well into the future. Loyal customers come back with repeat orders, time and time again.

Slow and inefficient processes, finished goods just sitting around and waiting for something to happen - all these add cost. Finding ways to cut down on these non-value added activities is the challenge and opportunity that a Lean Management System brings to a business. These types of waste are oftentimes referred to as the 'hidden factory' or unseen cost of 'doing business'. It is important for a business to be able to qualify and quantify the hidden waste. In doing this they will bring it to everyone's awareness and be able to focus on reducing it or eliminating it, which will improve the bottom line by cutting down on cost and waste. That is the heart and purpose of a Lean Management System.

Getting rid of things (even internal process steps, time, and inventory) that add no value to your customers is the number one priority of a Lean Management System. The costs of poor quality products, services, and waste, add up over time and could cause a business to lose their loyal customers and any potential repeat or new business. Really taking issue with these aspects can save money and time, to ensure customer retention and satisfaction. Customers want to do business with a provider that is reliable, fast and affordable, stable and predictable.

It is important to define expectations and to set targets in key areas of a business and to work diligently towards achieving them. The results will be evident to everyone and the changes will influence employees and customers alike to ensure these changes will 'stick' and be sustainable over time. Everyone will experience the motivation, and it can be infectious in very positive ways.

Every business that is implementing a Lean Management System must start by asking a key question: How long does it take to convert an order into a finished product and get it out of the door and into the hands of the customer? Is this lead time measured in seconds, minutes, hours, days, or weeks? Asking the question is important, because it raises awareness. It is putting a number to the lead time and quantifying it, which makes the process visible and measurable, and enables a business to do something about it! For example, it will allow them to define and set a target to show how much they want to reduce it. This will allow them to measure and track the progress to see if the process is actually being reduced over time.

The name of the game in a Lean Management System is to identify and eliminate waste to increase value for the customer. Any and all processes within a business are fair game for an improvement team providing they can increase value for the customer. If improving a process does not increase the value for the customer, then this type of improvement would be a low priority. Equally, improvement does not only have to be only focused on the manufacturing processes. Other examples could easily include: product development, order entries, design, customer service, HR, and financial processes as well.

By taking this 'overall' holistic approach towards improvement, a business is adding value and creating the potential to increase profits to benefit the bottom line. The business can do all this while streamlining and becoming a low-cost, reliable partner, and provider of choice.

Chapter 17

Metrics and Benefits

Taking an analytical approach to business will open everyone's eyes to new methods to grow, expand, strengthen, and position the business for results and success.

Ask the following questions to ascertain if a Lean Management System is right for an organization and if it has the potential to improve its business practices:

- Where is the real 'time' in our business spent?

- How much of this adds value to our customers?

- Is it worth it?

- Where can we make some changes?

- Is there any benefit in our business trying to establish a competitive edge getting goods and services to customers quicker?

- What kind of payback can we expect by implementing a Lean Management System? What are the financial benefits and potential here?

- If we cut operating expenses, manufacturing cost, overhead, inventory, lead, wait, and cycle times, how would it affect the bottom line?

- What would the financial impact be weekly, monthly, quarterly, annually? These metrics are critical to gauge the progress, raise awareness, and give a whole new outlook on where a business is doing well and which areas are in need of improvement.

- If we reduce our work in process (WIP) and finished goods inventory, what will that mean in financial terms to the business?

- What would the business be able to do with the additional cash at hand, that it is not able to do today? For example, capital investment, debt reduction, sales and marketing, etc.

- How will the savings from these changes benefit and grow the business?

When an organization is deploying a Lean Management System there are enabling aspects that a management team needs to pay attention to. Here are some of the operational and financial metrics they should take a close look at to help them answer some of the questions listed above:

- Operating margin.
- ROIC (return on investment capital).
- EBITDA (Earnings Before Interest, Taxes, Depreciation and Amortization)
- Capital Turnover.
- WIP (Work in Process).
- On-time delivery performance.
- Cost of poor quality.

- Quality performance.
- Customer satisfaction data.

Any executive management team or business owner that is focused on becoming the best in their industry by expanding market share and increasing profits must be able to answer these questions and establish metrics to guide their decision making. The simple rule of thumb that is central to a Lean Management System is that any improvements should benefit the customer and add value.

Implementing a Lean Management System does not mean that the management team is asking their employees to work harder or faster at the expense of manufacturing poor quality products. They are asking the employees to participate in the process to define the standard amount of time they need to create a quality product on a consistent and repeatable basis. A Lean Management System is asking for nothing more and nothing less than coming to an agreement of an acceptable standard. Once a standard has been clearly defined, it must be measured and tracked to determine if it is capable of meeting customer demand. If it cannot meet this goal, it will need an improvement team to identify why it is not capable of meeting customer demand.

Metrics are an important element of a Lean Management System because they make any time, quality, and cost issues within and in between processes, from start to finish, visible and tangible. Metrics gives eyes and ears to these processes and outcomes; it allows the management and employees to intervene to make things better to benefit the company and its customers. Metrics provide feedback to give purpose and direction, to develop a baseline, and to identify practical means to improve the results to bring about positive changes.

A Lean Management System should be a seamless operation that is not bureaucratic, and practices what it teaches by using lean principles to streamline its own internal processes. It must be able to integrate the goal of making business practices successful by increasing customer satisfaction. The overall methodology will help an organization re-make, re-energize, and re-shape its business culture into one that has a lean philosophy that is customer focused.

This approach allows the organization to make the shift from being re-active towards becoming a pro-active type of business. A pro-active business takes action using real-time data, and it is hands-on in its approach to problem solving. It does not leave success to chance, it uses real-time data to drive its decision making process. The real-time information influences the planning and executing of decisions based on the needs of the business to satisfy its customers day after day, month after month, and year after year.

One of the common issues that many companies experience when they start implementing a Lean Management System is the reduction of inventory. This is a good thing, however, when the financial statements start to surface after the first and second quarters there might be some push back from the CFO. Why is this?

Inventory is considered an asset on the profit and loss statement (P & L). If you reduce inventory levels it removes assets from the P & L statement which will reduce the amount of profit. Some CFO's will freak out about this because they want to see profits increasing, not decreasing. So the important question is this; "What happened to the inventory?"

Well, it was sold as goods to customers and converted into cash. The company is starting to get a tighter control on its inventory levels, therefore it will not have to purchase and replenish the same amount as before. As the inventory levels are reducing, the amount of cash in the organizations bank account will start increasing.

Chapter 18

Collaborate for Success

Agility, adaptability, low cost, and responsiveness are all qualities that an organization should have for doing business in today's economy. A prerequisite and entry-level requirement for this is the need to develop a Lean Management System. This will take a team approach, which will require everyone to actively participate in the process.

One of the great contributions that a Lean Management System brings to any business is that it defines what I would call 'shared purpose, direction, and goals'. This individual and mutual orientation and coordinated effort gives a common direction to all. It fosters a high level of commitment and camaraderie between all the employees. It strengthens and builds the organization, links the leaders to the shop-floor employees, and engages everyone at all levels to achieve improvements in performance. It is a unifying and motivational principle that will underpin and build the collaborative effort towards getting results quicker and maintaining them over time. This is a critical element towards making any success sustainable.

Management and employees must ask a question: How do they think a Lean Management System can help their company? They need to consider their options, determine the pros and cons of implementing it versus not implementing it, and then make a decision.

The best way to enable and strengthen any business is to use lean tools that are integrated into a Lean Management System. It will create the governance infrastructure and instill the discipline to drive improvements, reduce costs, and encourage lean thinking in all levels of the business to reap the maximum rewards. An organization with a strong governance process will always triumph over one that does not have one.

Other aspects to consider for deploying a Lean Management System in a business are as follows:

Leadership

Demonstrating initiative and leading by example from the top is the key to success. The main flag-bearers and champions of the Lean Management System must be the business leader (Owner, CEO, President, etc.) and the senior management team.

Buy-in and support can make or break the efforts of a Lean Management System. There must be a demonstration of personal, hands-on, practical engagement by all the management team. They must show their commitment through their own business practices.

They will need to consider, define, and present some type of rewards and recognition system for employees to demonstrate their full participation in the lean initiatives. Performance improvements must be a critical factor for the successful implementation of Lean Management System initiatives.

Inspire and Mobilize Others.

Support and championing of the Lean Management System efforts by the corporate business culture and infrastructure contributes to its momentum and success throughout the organization. Include and engage everyone. A Lean Management System provides an organization with the opportunity to harness and leverage the talents of the entire workforce and collective, not merely a hand-full of individuals or some key employees. Get everyone to participate and contribute!

If the ability to achieve results and sustain a high level of excellence in operational performance matters to you and your business, the means to achieve this are in the Lean Management System toolkit. If you want to improve something, then start with the performance metrics and reverse engineer them. Ask these questions: Why are you not achieving the right results? What is stopping this process from meeting the expected results?

Metrics drive behavior. Change the organization to practice the right behaviors by measuring the right things. Clearly defined goals and expectations make it easier to achieve positive change that will have an impact and reshape a business.

The right metrics drive the right behaviors!

The wrong metrics force people to focus on doing the wrong things, which is another form of waste!

Infrastructure, Support, and Deployment

A Lean Management System requires everyone to share in the commitment, discipline, and perseverance to get an organization to where it needs to be to achieve its North Star (or vision). The process starts with just a few people but it must expand to include everyone being involved.

The goal is to create an organizational philosophy that is customer focused. Everyone in the business, no matter what they are doing, whether it is planning, producing, improving, etc., knows what the customer wants. They understand how the customer defines value, why they want it, and how to get it to them quickly, effectively, consistently, and affordably, anytime, every time! To do this, an organization must undergo a paradigm shift and start to move their focus onto the needs of the customer.

Engage everyone in the process, assign roles and responsibilities, and tap into the full potential everyone has to bring to the table. Committed resources, time, and training (initial investment), will pay off quickly. Mobilize your workforce and enable, empower, and energize them.

Vision

Making it all about your customer is the key. They are your incoming revenue streams, what keeps the wheels of your business churning. Make it count! Create a vision for your company based on giving the customer what they want, when they want it. The vision defines where you are going as an organization. Get it right and you succeed. Get it wrong and you will fail.

Reducing variability in business practices is an essential part of implementing a Lean Management System. Being consistent, predictable, and reliable as a provider or supplier, or business partner is a priority. Never merely focus on reducing defects based on emotional responses to situations. Know why you are doing it and how it adds value to your customer(s).

Everyone in an organization has to understand the need for this mutual undertaking. They must be able to clearly define its value and the potential rewards it will bring to the business. Also, it is important to give recognition to the role and contribution of everyone's efforts and input.

Right Resources and Projects

A Lean Management System that has dedicated resources working exclusively to support the necessary processes, improvements, and projects will achieve more desirable outcomes and results. Meaningful performance improvement requires the right people, with the right resources, working on the right projects, to increase value within a business. Successful improvement activities must be customer focused and deliberately targeted to increase value. Improvement projects that cannot increase value for the customer use valuable resources and this is another form of waste.

Teamwork

It is important to get everyone in the organization to understand their role and responsibilities. Employees need to know what is expected of them and how they fit into the process.

Management, shop-floor, administrative, and all staff members should be allowed to participate. They can all contribute to make a difference.

Managers should set the example when their organization is implementing a Lean Management System. If they do this, they will help to get the ball rolling. They should demonstrate their commitment to the process by providing support and encouragement along the way. Direction and results matter and are critical to the success of the process. It will require an organization to identify champions and process leaders and get them involved in the improvement process. They will be responsible for oversight of specific projects, allocating resources, and getting results.

Training and coaching will be required to get everyone to understand the lean principles and how they are applied in a Lean Management System. Once everybody understands the process, they will need to get involved in data collection, analysis, and problem-solving to find solutions and implement them to improve the process. All this takes an investment in time and resources, but it is well worth the effort and cost. If an organization makes this investment, they will reap huge rewards. Many companies see benefits that exceed their expectations in as little as 1 year! In fact, some businesses will see results in less time if they follow the correct process and implement the right Lean Management System infrastructure.

Culture and Technology

Lean technology and lean culture go hand in hand, and an organization must use and develop both to succeed. Most companies make the mistake of jumping in and focusing on implementing lean tools. However, this might not be the most appropriate or effective way of unleashing the power of Lean on any organization. A Lean Management System is not simply a matter of learning and implementing lean tools. If this were the case, a manufacturing business could become a lean manufacturing company overnight we know from history that this is not true. It is more than just implementing lean tools, it is about creating the right environment or culture.

It is critical to get the commitment to put the right infrastructure in place to support the Lean Management System. Without this, an organization cannot prepare their employees, plan for success, designate people, and allocate resources, etc. Developing the right culture will save lots of time and money and reduce the headaches down the line when it comes to actually doing the work and implementing the improvements.

It is important not to kid ourselves at this point in the process. Implementing a Lean Management System takes time, it requires discipline and planning. Planning for success in any Lean Management System deployment is essential. An organization must pay close attention and ensure they have the right metrics to measure the performance of their processes. The Lean Management System paradigm is having the best infrastructure and support in place so that everyone is prepared and trained. They know when it is appropriate to use specific lean tools and they understand how to use them.

Making It The Way You Do Business!

A Lean Management System is not only about projects! It is about so much more than that. It goes deeper and beyond. It is and will become the way that an organization does business. Everything a business undertakes in their Lean Management System must start with the customer. They need to find out who they are, what they want, and how they can get it to them quickly. The system must be able to deliver the products or services to specification, in working order, at an affordable price, and delivered on-time, every time. Sounds like a tall order, right?

Well, research shows that 21st century customers know what they want and when they want it. They are informed and empowered and demand the same from their suppliers. To stay profitable and thrive in the 21st century marketplace a business must understand what its customers are requesting. They must get in line with what their customers are demanding and begin to search for ways to deliver their products or services in the most cost effective and efficient manner.

An effective Lean Management System starts with an action plan, the right culture, and deploying the best lean technology to unleash its power and rewards on a business and its customers.

By now, I hope you have reached the conclusion that a Lean Management System can help to identify and eliminate waste to increase value for the customer. It achieves this by delivering what customers want, when they want it, reducing costs and improving quality.

Let's switch gears and look at specific areas where a Lean Management System can help an organization and their customers. Where can they have the most impact on the business so that it makes a difference?

Wait times and cycle times from start to finish all impact business success. The secret is that a Lean Management System is not just for manufacturing processes. It can be applied to all business processes.

Chapter 19

Change Through Improvement

Many organizations over extend themselves to a point that they end up improving little to nothing. Why and how do they do this? It is because most management teams are fragmented in their knowledge of the business processes and they do not fully understand the capabilities and limitations of their organization. It is important to be realistic about a company's ability to affect positive change. Change has to be promoted, planned, and managed. Sadly, many managers believe it can happen with little to no input from them personally. The change process is often delegated to a lower level employee that is given the responsibility for finding solutions to problems but has no power to implement them.

Another problem is the availability of people to participate and support the improvement process. A manager has to keep their business processes working to meet the delivery schedule for customer orders. Given the choice, is the manager going to focus on keeping the lines running? Or are they going to impact their production schedules by sending one or more of their people to participate as a team member in a rapid improvement (Kaizen) event? The manager knows that his employees will probably be taken out of the production process for several days. What is the incentive for the manager to release their employees?

Managers must be aware of and understand the improvement process and how much employees learn during each team event. This learning process is an essential part of the cultural exchange between all the team members and the facilitator.

Once the team members acquire this additional information and learning experience they can take it back to their own work areas and apply it. The potential for improvement grows with every employee that experiences a rapid improvement (Kaizen) event. The more employees that develop a clear acceptance of the value of being a team member in an improvement team, the more ideas they bring back to their workplace. So, the incentive for a manager is clear. The more employees they can put forward to be part of an event, the more they can integrate the experiences of each employee to improve their departmental processes. It creates what is called "group synergy." This is when the productivity of a group is greater than the sum of the capability of each individual.

Knowing where to focus the valuable resources such as time, people, equipment, etc., is critically important. However, the perfect method to identify the perfect project does not exist. An organization will need to develop the ability to work with whatever data and information it has available in the moment. Decision making has at its core an inherent level of risk; sometimes you get it right, but sometimes you are going to fail. When deploying a Lean Management System into an organization, the management team had better get used to the idea of failure and using it to their advantage. One technique that can help to reduce the level of risk is the "Pareto Principle or the 80/20 rule."

Using the 80/20 rule with a Lean Management System is a handy tool to help prioritize and focus on which areas of the business need to be improved right away. The 80/20 rule says that "80% of the problems or potential for improvement is hidden within 20% of the process." It is the job of an improvement team to collect and analyze data to determine which 20% of the process is hiding the 80% of the problems or potential to improve it. It is important to point out that both manufacturing and transactional processes can benefit from using this approach.

A Lean Management System can apply the 80/20 rule to any and all processes.

- Supply Chain Management (SCM)
- Logistics
- Manufacturing
- Design Processes
- Transactional
- Other

The common tool that is most often used to identify the 80/20 ratio in any business process is called "A Pareto Chart," see an example in Fig 23. A Pareto Chart allows an improvement team to identify the '*vital few*' issues (20%) that are creating most (80%) of the waste.

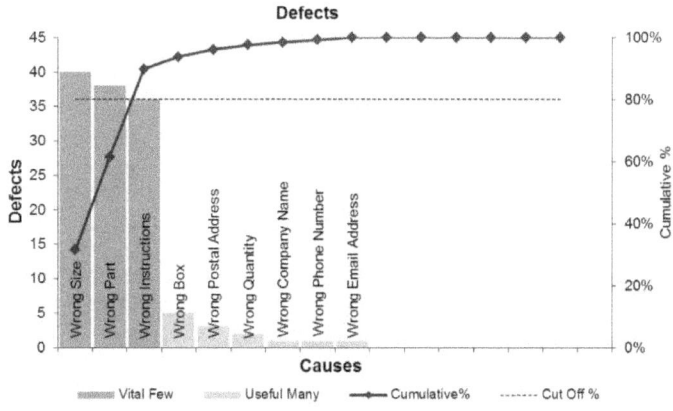

Fig 23: Pareto Chart.

99

Once the team knows which specific activities are causing the problem they can focus their time and energy on finding solutions to eliminate them. This is one way of getting the '*best bang for the buck*' and using valuable resources in an effective way.

So far, we have discovered that a Lean Management System can be defined as:

"A business management philosophy that requires a paradigm shift in the way its employees think about and perform their work activities to deliver their products or services to their customers on time, every time."

It stems from a proud history and is grounded in the quality improvement movement developed by the Japanese auto industry, before spreading to Europe and the West. Total Quality Management (TQM) initiatives and key principles from the Toyota Production System (TPS) improve quality, time and cost metrics, by shifting the focus onto the identification and elimination of waste.

Getting rid of the main sources of waste in any business means paying attention to the following:

- Over-production

- Waiting

- Transportation

- Over Processing

- Excessive Inventory

100

- Excessive Motion

- Defects

- Underutilized People

There are some basic tools that must be made available in the Lean Management System toolkit. These tools are mentioned in the 10 Steps to become a Lean Enterprise model and they will get any business off to a good start. The most important thing is to use them on a consistent basis so employees learn and become comfortable when using them.

Here are the 10 Steps again for your reference:

Step 1 – Strategy Deployment

Step 2 – Value Stream Mapping

Step 3 – Workplace Organization

Step 4 – Improve Process Flow

Step 5 – Reduce Changeover Times

Step 6 – Implement a Pull System

Step 7 – Balanced Workload

Step 8 – Standard Work

Step 9 – Continuous Process Improvement

Step 10 – Lean Supply Chain

As an organization starts to reach a level of maturity in their Lean Management System they will start to expand their knowledge of the tools and techniques to support their improvement process. They may even start to incorporate other improvement systems such as Six Sigma or Theory of

Constraints into their Lean Management System. It is an organic and dynamic process that changes as the culture of the organization changes to accommodate the new methods. An organization should never be satisfied with the status quo! If they are, they are standing still and not improving their processes to reflect the needs of their customers. A company that does this is doomed to fail. Without positive growth, there is no positive future!

The logic and rationale behind the premise for implementing a Lean Management System states that by reducing the waste, you are improving quality. At the same time, the production cycle times and costs are being reduced. The primary focus of any Lean Management System is "People First!" Without the full support of the employees and their willingness to participate in the lean improvement process, it will be doomed to failure.

Kaizen is a Japanese term and it is at the very heart of any lean improvement process. A Lean Management System can be implemented into any industry or business field, such as manufacturing, healthcare, or administration companies that have transactional processes. Some, any, or all of the processes involved in these businesses can be included in a Lean Management System deployment and initiatives.

The key lean principles can be identified as:

- Getting it right the first time with no defects and identifying and solving problems from the source quickly and as they happen

- Non-value added elimination and optimizing all resources at your disposal

- Kaizen (or on-going Continuous Process Improvement (CPI) as it is also known) - continuing to raise the bar of performance and excellence in your business. This can be achieved through a Lean Management System focused on reducing costs by improving quality, increasing productivity and better information sharing, streamlined operations, and great teamwork that uses focused, targeted process improvement techniques.

- Customer-demand drives activity in a pull not push system and inventory; wait times etc., are effectively reduced and even eliminated where possible.

- Efficient systems that are adaptable, agile, and have flexibility without reducing quality.

- Extending these efficiencies and efforts into your supply chain and other business partnerships in a collaborative effort, building relationships that fit, work, and last.

It is like having a recipe for achieving success in the new global, fast-paced, technology enabled and driven, highly competitive marketplace and economy. Using the Lean Management System way and tools better enables and empowers you and your business to not only succeed in this environment, but flourish and thrive!

Its history and future is built on the premise that wasted, time, space, energy, effort, money, and poor quality, all cost money and should be made visible, dealt with, and eliminated. A Lean Management System quickly sets a business on the path towards success through improvement. It does this by allowing everyone to work quicker with less effort and with the minimum amount of waste, cost, and time. It is also more than merely focusing on manufacturing processes. There is more to the philosophy and methodology than meets the eye.

Think of innovative ways to cut costs in your business and operation without risk to productivity, quality, employees, or customers. Eliminate and trim unnecessary process steps, cheaper alternatives, or costly extras that are not really necessary. Shared utility or tools are a great way to minimize expenses, set-up times, and overall costs. Make the most the resources that you have available today.

Take a closer look at the materials and processes you and your team use every day and try to spot the "as is" process.
Do a reality check. See the costs and waste, put metrics to things, raise awareness of what could be done differently, more effectively, and cheaper. Sometimes process steps can be eliminated or combined to give a better use of resources to deliver quick results.

Standardization goes a long way to cut down on waste. Take a close look at instances where you are tweaking and adjusting machines for no apparent reason other than routine and habit. This practice will need to be stopped. Reuse, reduce, and recycle comes into play. Implementing more effective process steps that take less time will help your business grow faster. Do some research and see if technology, automation, outsourcing etc., can help you and your customers save time and money.
Take action to correct certain aspects within your business. Get rid of waste and streamline processes for optimal function and ultimate success; this is what a Lean Management System is all about. As I have said many times throughout this book, a lean

methodology is a process of learning by doing and requires a hands-on approach. It engages and energizes people. It sparks interest and builds involvement and the need to take action. Looking for new opportunities is an ongoing cycle. It includes making changes, reviewing the results and adapting if necessary, then celebrating your success.

Chapter 20

Lean Management System

A Lean Management System is an easy way to put in place the fundamental practices in your business right away. Too many organizations put it off, waiting for the right time. The right time is today because the more you wait the longer it will take you to reduce the waste.

Remember, the cost of the waste in your business practices is included in the purchase price of your product or service. The person that is paying for this waste is the customer. So, an important question to ask is: "If your customers knew they were paying to support your wasteful practices, would they continue to do business with your company?" The answer is: "No, they would not." They would find another supplier to support their needs.

Kai-Zen or 'change for the better' is the mantra for a Lean Management System. It is an on-going and never ending process. By effectively focusing on improving the efficiency and effectiveness of any underlying processes and improving performance, a business will reap the financial rewards. Customer satisfaction is a true measure of success because satisfied customers keep coming back with repeat business. Dissatisfied customers do not come back, and what is worse, they tell other business owners about their experience.

By bringing practical, intuitive and creative problem-solving, analysis, and scrutiny to business processes, you increase the amount of control you have in the unfolding events, steps, and outcomes. It drives the performance excellence of your business to new heights. A Lean Management System will help you to get there quickly. Combining this approach with the discipline and rigor of process management and business process improvement tools will increase the impact and effectiveness of your business practices.

There are three pillars or areas of focus for this type of business approach:

(i) Customer centric activity, with value-add process and outcome

(ii) Operational Effectiveness

(iii) Performance Excellence (PEx).

Customer Centric Activity

A business owner or management team must define how they are going to move towards a customer centric organization. The question to ask is: Are our process activities customer focused? The answer is a simple Yes or No! The processes are customer focused or they are not, there is no grey area or in-between state.

Giving customers exactly what they want and exceeding their expectations is important. Why would a customer choose your company? What is your business specialty that will set you apart from the crowd? It is a world of multiple choices when it comes to a customer choosing a supplier.

Again, some self-diagnostics from the Lean Management System toolkit will help you out regarding assessing your own business and readiness:

- How can a Lean Management System help you establish, identify, and communicate that competitive edge to your business employees, partners, and customers?

- How successful are your products and services in securing 'clients for life' and repeat business? How strong is your brand?

- How do you currently minimize costs, reduce operating expenses, and deal with waste?

- How does your organization deal with problems and customer feedback?

Yet another essential Lean Management System tool and utility to consider is something referred to as Total Productive Maintenance (TPM). This is different from routine or occasional maintenance that has to be performed. Having no downtime and scheduled maintenance as a result of pro-active planning, as opposed to a more re-active approach is recommended in the Lean Management System philosophy and its practical application.

TPM is often depicted as "deterioration prevention." It is not focused on fixing machines when they break down. There is much more involved in the TPM process. Equipment must be ready at any and all times to meet operational needs. The equipment should be able to provide efficiency on demand, while running and providing a quality service and output.

Overall Equipment Effectiveness (OEE) uses three key performance metrics: quality, availability (or uptime), and throughput, to track the performance of the equipment. OEE will gage how the maintenance tasks are meeting the demands of the manufacturing processes. It will give valuable feedback about what should be done, when it should be done, and who should do it to keep the equipment working continuously to meet customer demand. Mistake-proofing is important part of the TPM process. It will help to reduce variability, while increasing process capability.

Throughout this book I have provided examples and reasoning for why a Lean Management System will be good for any business, regardless of size or current level of performance. The lean tools and techniques demonstrated in this book can help you move your business forward. An underestimated factor in all Lean Management System deployments is the underutilized talents of our collective and collaborative potential. We oftentimes get so busy with what each of us are doing individually, that we lose sight of how much more powerful we could be if we combined our efforts. The team approach is the best method for improvement because the collective wisdom of many is more powerful than the wisdom of one.

In my opinion, here-in lies the secret of Lean Management System …

We have to give everyone the opportunity to partake and participate, share in the experience and undertaking for maximum results!

Ask yourself how you can make the most of people's time and investment in the Lean Management System practices and how it will benefit your business? Your resources, employees, and customers are important assets – how are you using and utilizing them to become a more agile and cost-effective operation? Always start by asking what can I do? This personal hands-on approach can truly make a difference in any business.

Here is a list of ways to avoid your Lean Management System initiatives from being thwarted, failing, or coming up short:

- Pay special and close attention to what the business culture really is! It could be totally out of alignment with the principles and fundamentals of a Lean Management System and this will cause some stress that will develop into resistance within and throughout the organization.

- Ask your team, business partners, and customers what the existing climate is that would support lean methods and how it will benefit all stakeholders?

- Here is another useful question: Is your organization hierarchical, rigid and autocratic, and not a people centered company?

- Ask: Are you learning what not to do from the mistakes and discoveries, shared learning, and insights?

- Be aware that not everyone will necessarily share your enthusiasm for a Lean Management System. Some might dread what it does to their work load and environment. Some initial resistance to any change is normal. Showing the value or the WIIFM (what is in it for me) is a very important part of the whole Lean Management System.

Here are ten easy tips of how to enable a Lean Management System in your organization:

1. Keep the channels of communication open!
   - Talk and inform often.

   - Educate and empower, knowledge, skill, practice and competence, on-going mastery, and teaching others.

   - Trust, honesty, and information = transparency.

   - Give everyone a head start, a common language, goal, and purpose, and unleash the power of lean on your organization.

2. Give opportunity for everyone for input and feedback!
   - Get everyone engaged, excited, and hands-on involved and aboard with your Lean Management System initiatives and plans

   - Introduce feedback and coaching, establishing communication channels where before there might have been none.

3. Create and cultivate the right working environment!
   - Set communication and information sharing, learning and openness (transparency), as an organizational priority

- Less people will feel threatened and insecure about speaking up, or hiding errors for fear of embarrassment or consequences (like being held accountable or losing their jobs or face in front of others)

- Treat each other with respect, and share ideas and issues openly, always keeping in mind the overall benefit (or detriment) for all if closer attention is paid to certain issues or challenges at hand.

4. Take notice, reward, encourage, and celebrate!
- Select examples of great achievement with Lean Management System case studies. Share and celebrate them all-round. Give credit and recognition to the team where it is due, for accomplishments that made a great difference for the company, a specific area, or problem that was solved. It is highly motivational and quite an incentive for many to keep trying and do more!

5. Implement a system of metrics and monitor process!
- Formalized record and tracking is essential for these Lean Management System processes and initiative to work and last! Ensure they are streamlined and purposeful, organized, and occur regularly.

6. Stick to the basics and keep it simple!
- It sounds easy enough to make things simple, but believe me it is easy to get sidetracked with the day to day issues.

- It is easy to become overwhelmed by the deluge of data and information, the intricacies of calculations, metrics and spreadsheets, that we often forget the release of pressure and clarity that simplicity brings.

- Making things easy to learn and follow is the best improvement!

7. Stay positive and keep at it!
   - Understand that things will go wrong. Not one business is capable of implementing a Lean Management System without experiencing problems, along the way!

   - Problems are results or outcomes. They are feedback from the system telling you that something is not performing to plan. Take notice and investigate, then find ways to improve the process!

8. Achieve and tap into your resources!
   - Be always focused on needs, wants, desires, and motivations, to mobilize and sustain momentum and change.

   - Make the stake and reward personal for participating and applying the principles of a Lean Management System.

   - Make it the way that you do business – without compromise!

   - Set the bar and standards high and keep on reaching higher.

9. Disciplined practice!
   - Be consistent, persistent, determined, and dedicated to make things work, better, and last!

- Search for better ways to become a low cost, no waste, effective and efficient business!

- Understand that the path to success in any Lean Management System is to make the shift from optional to required behaviors. It requires a high level of internal discipline to allow this to happen!

10. Lean is a continuing journey!
   - Ongoing learning is an essential part of the lean journey. It is important to continue learning from our mistakes, oversights, challenges, and achievements.

   - Practice Hansei (reflection). Always asking what we learned, what went well, what did not work, and how can we make it all better the next time around, should be part of normal conversation and routine.

   - Never accept the status quo. Always know that there is yet another level of improvement beyond that which you see today. This is the true meaning of Kai-Zen!

Always remember, despite what you read or hear from consultants, there is no one-size fits all Lean Management System deployment that works and fits for everyone. It depends on the organization, leadership, dynamics, etc.

Much has been written about lean principles (see reference listing for an eclectic sampling of some recent books and classics on the topic). Practical information on how to implement lean, especially in a small business is hard to come by. Tapping into the expertise of those who have walked this path is a great way to discover the secrets and pitfalls, and mistakes to avoid when considering implementing a Lean Management System for your organization.

Start by asking what the current readiness and knowledge levels regarding lean would be? Even though many have heard about lean principles, they do not realize how little they really know until they start to implement them. For some, lean thinking comes naturally. While for others, it is a little more demanding to ensure success and requires discipline to effect and impact business processes.

Are you currently implementing lean principles to cut down on waste, scrap, or unnecessary costs? Remember, over 90% of companies that embark on a lean journey will not be doing anything associated with lean practices by the end of their second year. What is the main reason? A lack of internal discipline!

There is always room for improvement in any business. A Lean Management System provides the tools and means, channels, and connections to plan, execute and sustain these changes to benefit your customers and employees, profits, and bottom line. Always remember this…

You cannot do or achieve your goals and objectives overnight. You need the combined efforts and buy-in, support and infrastructure to get things done, and it may take longer than expected. The important thing is to stick with it. Rome was not built in a day!

A Lean Management System is an on-going journey and not a 'quick-fix' for business woes! However, some of the tools and applications will start to make a measurable difference and deliver immediate rewards and benefits. Dedicated time and resources, and focused and targeted effort will increase the benefits from your Lean Management System initiatives. Shift your focus to more long-term, and step out of the day-to-day fire-fighting that is typically found in most organizations. They are dealing with one problem at a time as they come up, and they are not following a very effective strategy overall. A Lean Management System is about more than tools, counterintuitive thinking, and application to manufacturing and transactional processes! It is about the people involved in, touched by, working with and through these processes and outcomes, to improve and sustain business success and growth.

Someone once quipped that lean is not about what you see, but comes from what you think. The impetus and motivation starts early and it starts with each of us. Engage and enable the minds and hearts of your people and mobilize your organization, taking it to new heights of performance excellence and increasing bottom line profit. Tap into the collective talents within your organization, become more organic, lead by example, and emphasize that this is not a program (with a start and finish date). This is an initiative that will continue, grow, and expand from here on forward.

Things cannot and will not stay the same with the deployment of a Lean Management System – that is the one guarantee you can count on.

Skill-building, training, knowledge-application, refinement, and mastery will come over time. There will be learning curves, which will be steep at the beginning but over time things will get easier. There is no specific recipe for implementing lean principles, just some general directions. We can use these to create a roadmap, which includes general ideas and suggestions, like those mentioned in this book, to achieve success.

In the lean principles toolbox, it is not about how many tools you can deploy, but how you unleash, utilize, and leverage them! I have covered several key lean tools to get you started implementing a Lean Management System. However, there a hundreds of tools available and it will take time to develop competency to master these as part of your overall strategy for improving a business.

Jidoka, kaizen, andon, kanban, SMED, visual management, 5S, 5 Whys, are all examples of lean tools that you can use. It all starts with how we think about things and the shift that we have to make in our minds from conventional, traditional, and current ways of doing things. It is important to figure out and understand what does and does not work.

A Lean Management System starts with each employee and a willingness to be open minded, see, discover, and harness the potential savings, cost, and waste reduction opportunities within and across the organization. This includes business partners and customers because to become successful and better at what you do, they must become better at what they do without sacrificing quality.

Here is an example of what I mean. When an organization eliminates waste and speeds up their manufacturing processes, they will reduce their inventory levels and need their suppliers to replenish them on a regular basis. To continue to deliver products to their customer's on-time, every time, an organization must get their suppliers and business partners to improve the delivery processes to match their own manufacturing speed or customer demand. If their supplier fails to deliver on-time, every time, they will fail to deliver to their own customers too.

Mastering a tool like the 5S (reducing waste or muda), you could go around cleaning up basically, without a detailed understanding or internalizing the ability to immediately identify problems. No advanced Lean Management System tool will help us do that and come magically to the rescue like a 'silver bullet' to enable quick responses. What then would be the purpose? Can you see the difference?

For those of us who would want to learn more about a Lean Management System and the tools that can be applied with great success in your business, consider these four rules adapted from Bowen and Spears in "Decoding the DNA of the Toyota Production System" (Harvard Business Review, Nov. 1999).

Here is an overview of the Four Rules:

The Four Rules

The tacit knowledge that underlies the Toyota Production System can be captured in four basic rules. These rules guide the design, operation, and improvement of every activity, connection, and pathway for every product and service. The rules are as follows:

Rule 1: *All work shall be highly specified as to content, sequence, timing and outcome.*

Rule 2: *Every customer-supplier connection must be direct, and there must be an unambiguous yes-or-no way to send requests and receive responses.*

Rule 3: The pathway for every product and service must be single and direct.

Rule 4: Any improvement must be made in accordance with the scientific method, under the guidance of a teacher, at the lowest possible level in the organization.

All the rules require that activities, connections, and flow paths have built-in tests to signal problems automatically. It is the continual response to problems that makes this seemingly rigid system so flexible and adaptable to changing circumstances.

In Kanban for example, it is not about the visual cue or tool as much as understanding the logic and importance of upstream and downstream process flow and the implications for operations and customers.

Decision-making, problem-solving, and management will be affected and enabled by this type of thinking, and very soon it will be about so much more than mere application of tools on a couple of projects. It will change the way you think about and do business moving forward, forever!

Chapter 21

A Lean Toolbox Overview

A quick summary is provided here of some of the most basic Lean Management System 'tools' to get you off to a good start. They are:

5S
- Sort, Set in Order, Shine, Standardize and Sustain.
- Identifies what is needed and what is not needed.
- Organizes the needed items into specific locations. A place for everything and everything in its place.
- Create a visual environment to allow employees to identify problems quickly.

5 Whys
- It is a problem-solving technique.
- Ask "Why" the problem occurred.
- Keep asking "Why" to eliminate the symptoms of the problem.
- Repeat the process five times to get to the 'root cause' of a problem.

Visual management
- Purpose is to manage every aspect of the process by visual means.
- Identify the process status at a glance.
- The most common visual indicators are lines, labels, and signs.

Andon
- Operator pulls a cord that triggers a signal such as a horn or flashing light, which indicates a specific condition.
- For example, it may indicate to a supervisor or team lead that an employee needs help or support.
- Its primary use is to keep production processes moving and to give an early warning of potential problems.

Jidoka
- Autonomation or identifying problems prior to proceeding or moving the product onto the next step.
- The process will either be stopped by an employee to correct the problem or it can be an automated machine that has the capability of self-correcting the issue.

Kaizen
- A continuous improvement process.
- Engages those closest to the process.
- Its purpose is to improve both the effectiveness and efficiency of the process
- Small incremental changes over time with a focus on eliminating waste and standardization.

Kanban
- A signal or card system that a downstream (customer) process can use to indicate a specific replenishment need.
- It is usually triggered when the inventory level has been lowered to a pre-defined quantity.
- It is optimized to signal a request for a defined quantity of a specific part from an upstream (supply) process.

Single Minute Exchange of Die - SMED

- Focused on equipment downtime because of product changeovers.
- Involves a structured process to identify the waste.
- Speeds up the changeover process, reduces downtime and increases the amount of production time.
- Creates a standardized changeover process to track the equipment uptime.

A lean toolbox will start off with a couple of tools. As you become proficient at using them, you will learn to implement additional lean tools. Do not make the common mistake of being a "jack of all trades and a master of none!" It is a more effective approach to successfully implement a few tools and get good results. There is nothing more frustrating or deflating than seeing a lack of results because you are trying to do too much, with little to no experience.

Chapter 22

Conclusion

Getting on board with a Lean Management System is no easy task, but the initiative will soon deliver rewards to your business. Fostering its growth and allowing it to filter through all levels of the organization will definitely pay off in the long run.

Many organizations are so busy getting 'work' done, dealing with problems and putting out fires, meeting goals and objectives, and initiating business strategies, that they do not even consider taking the time to 'look' for waste. We should pause and take a minute to consider how lean principles, tools, and thinking can help us to eliminate waste. First, start by asking a question. "Am I focused on the important or the urgent?"

A Lean Management System is not focused on the "urgent," it is focused on the "important," and that means getting things to be in the right place at the right time, on-time, every time. When an organization is focused on the "urgent" it is because the system failed to deliver the right thing to the right place, at the right time. A continuous state of urgency cannot create the right environment to improve any business processes. It forces the people in the company to support the status quo, which initiates a downward spiral of denial into a state of business atrophy.

An organization must train all their employees to become "problem solvers." Problem solving must become part of their everyday business practices. Knowing how to analyze the situation and get to the root-cause makes process improvement easier. This process is on-going and will reveal things about your business you did not even know at all! You might be surprised by what you find, unearth, and reveal when using lean thinking and problem solving tools.

Looking at processes to see how to eliminate the different forms of muda or waste requires a new way of thinking, which at times will seem counterintuitive. It is imperative that everyone in a business start to move away from a traditional point of view to embrace a lean way of thinking and doing.

Here is an amazing truth, and in my opinion another key to really understanding the power and potential of a Lean Management System for businesses, regardless of their size, industry, challenges, and the like. The skill to recognize and understand the systems that create results is not a natural ability. No organization has an automatic and inbuilt lean process-focused capability. If they did there would be no need for lean training and implementation procedures. An organization has to train its people to discover through observation, develop through analysis, and refine their business practices to create the environment for a Lean Management System.

See value through the eyes of your customers and take a long hard look at what and how you are doing things to get them what they want, when they need it. Look for opportunities to improve value for the customer and reduce waste to lower cost, but remember – keep it simple. As the level of complexity increases, so does the cost because it is much more difficult to maintain the standard practices.

Everything that does not add value is waste and increases cost! In other words, if you are not adding value, you are adding cost. You cannot have it both ways. You must choose one or the other. I hope you choose to add value and reduce cost!

I wish you all the best on your lean journey. If you would like to learn more about lean principles, please visit my lean training and certification website called "Lean Certification Online" at www.leancertificationonline.com

Also, see the additional listing of lean resources and books that I have provided.

Reference and Resource List

For your reference, convenience and review here is a list of books with a focus on Lean Manufacturing Principles:

1. Ohno, Taiichi (1988), Toyota Production System: Beyond Large-Scale Production, Productivity Press, ISBN 0915299143

2. Womack, James P., Jones, Daniel T., and Roos, Daniel(1991), The Machine That Changed the World: The Story of Lean Production, Harper Perennial, ISBN0060974176

3. Womack, James P. and Jones, Daniel T. (1998), Lean Thinking Free Press, ISBN 0743249275.

4. Emiliani, B, with Stec, D., Grasso, L. and Stodder, J.(2007), Better Thinking, Better Results, Center for Lean Business Management LLC, ISBN 0972259120

5. Imai, Masaaki (1997), Gemba Kaizen, McGraw-Hill, ISBN 0070314462

6. Rother, Mike and Shook, John (1999), Learning to See, Lean Enterprise Institute, ISBN 0966784308

7. Schonberger, Richard J. (1986), World Class Manufacturing, Free Press, ISBN 0029292700

8. Levinson, William A. (2002), Henry Ford's Lean Vision: Enduring Principles from the First Ford Motor Plant, Productivity Press, ISBN 1563272601

9. Levinson, William A. and Rerick, Raymond (2002), Lean Enterprise: A Synergistic Approach to Minimizing Waste, ASQ Quality Press, ISBN 0873895320

10. Liker, Jeffrey (2003), The Toyota Way: 14 Management Principles from the World's Greatest

Manufacturer, First edition, McGraw-Hill, ISBN 0071392319.

11. Liker, Jeffrey (2005), The Toyota Way Fieldbook, First edition, McGraw-Hill, ISBN 0071448934.

12. Ford, Henry and Crowther, Samuel (2003), My Life and Work, Kessinger Press, ISBN 0766127745

13. Ford, Henry and Crowther, Samuel (1988), Today and Tomorrow, Productivity Press, ISBN 0915299364

14. Ford, Henry and Crowther, Samuel (2003), Moving Forward, Kessinger Press, ISBN 0766143392

15. Dinero, Donald (2005), Training Within Industry: The Foundation of Lean", Productivity Press, ISBN 1563273071

16. Imai, Masaaki (1986), Kaizen: The Key to Japan's Competitive Success, McGraw-Hill/Irwin, ISBN007554332X

17. Hirano, Hiroyuki (1995), 5 Pillars of the Visual Workplace, Productivity Press, ISBN 1563271230

Online Resources and Links:

1. Lean Certification Online – A premier online lean training and certification business. Online courses for Manufacturing, Healthcare and Administration. Chris Turner designed and developed the training curriculum for this website.
http://www.leancertificationonline.com/

2. Lean Manufacturing Coach – This is Chris Turner's Lean Consulting business website at
http://www.leanmfgcoach.com

3. Wikipedia – Lean Manufacturing
http://en.wikipedia.org/wiki/Lean_manufacturing

4. Wikipedia – Toyota Production System
http://en.wikipedia.org/wiki/Toyota_Production_System

5. NWLEAN: http://www.nwlean.net/- The North West Lean Networks - A free knowledge-sharing website, with over 10,000 professionals discussing the various aspects of lean implementation.

6. Lean Enterprise Institute (LEI) – They have an excellent Lean knowledge center athttp://www.lean.org/

About the Author

 Chris Turner grew up in a coal mining town in England. To his mother's chagrin, he would dis-assemble and re-assemble household appliances to see if they would work.

In college, Chris studied Mechanical Engineering. He then transitioned into Industrial Engineering. In 1983, he was introduced to the concept of 'Just in Time' (JIT). He became a lean consultant and gained experience working with clients, including top business organizations in the UK.

In 1996, Chris and his wife moved to the United States. He continued his career in the continuous process improvement field. Chris designed, and developed the '10 Steps to become a Lean Enterprise' training model and went on to establish a successful online lean training business called 'Lean Certification Online.' He created the online self-paced courses for people to learn about the application of lean principles in three key business fields Manufacturing, Administration and Healthcare.

For those who took the time to read this page, remember this quote:

"Knowing is not enough, we must apply.
Willing is not enough, we must do."
- *Johann Wolfgang von Goethe*

www.ingramcontent.com/pod-product-compliance
Lightning Source LLC
Chambersburg PA
CBHW051322170526
45166CB00002B/648